THE BACK HOME SERIES

SERIES TITLES

Soul of the Outdoors
Dave Greschner

From the Heart: The Story of Matrix
John Harmon

The Long Fields
Anne-Marie Oomen

Kick Out the Bottom
Erik Mortenson & Christopher Kramer

Wrong Tree: Adventures in Wildlife Biology
Jeff Wilson

At the Lake
Jim Landwehr

Body Talk
Takwa Gordon

The In-Between State
Martha Lundin

North Freedom
Carolyn Dallmann

Ohio Apertures
Robert Miltner

An Ignorance of Trees

To an essential catalogue of poems, Jim Daniels adds these essays—prose meditations, tests, and intimate measures—on life's riddles and mysteries. A more than worthy work in words. Bravo.

—THOMAS LYNCH
National Book Award Finalist
author of *The Depositions* and *Bone Rosary*

As with his poetry and fiction, Jim Daniels' essays contain a compelling combination of swagger and vulnerability. The swagger is never self-aggrandizing, and the vulnerability is tempered by his Detroit working-class upbringing, which underpins his work. His prose—alternately hard-edged and lyric—reflects this dichotomy. He embodies the famous quote widely attributed to Hemingway, "There is nothing to writing. All you do is sit down at a typewriter and bleed." Daniels is probably the most introspective and sensitive tough guy writing today.

—SUE WILLIAM SILVERMAN
author of How to Survive Death and Other Inconveniences

"What can I say . . . to keep you from being as bored as you would be looking through my family calendar, crossing off the days?" writes Jim Daniels in his excellent, poignant essay "The Family Calendar." What he says in every essay in *An Ignorance of Trees* is plain spoken and honest, conversational and well observed, grounded and vulnerable—all the adjectives that describe writing that feels so authentic that nowhere is the reader bored in this page-turner of a book that memorably shows both the joys and regrets that make a memoir authentic and moving.

—GARY FINCKE
author of *The Darkness Call* and *The Mayan Syndrome*

The magical backyard swing set of Jim Daniels' working-class Detroit childhood offered two options. There were the real swings, those rubber-seated, rusty-chained wonders that stained kids' hands orange but promised flight to those who pumped their legs hard enough and were brave enough to let go. And there was the glide ride—that safe and dull alternative that swayed from side to side, limited in both movement and its ability to spark dreams. Throughout *An Ignorance of Trees*, Daniels' latest gift, the author brilliantly weaves a tapestry of worlds—the world he was born into and the worlds that, over decades of risk and loss, of heartbreak and joy, he made his own. Here we find factories and workers forever stuck on the glide-ride. Here we encounter people who grew up knowing the names of cars and not the names of trees.

This book is a beautiful meditation on what changes and what we keep. It's a meditation on a childhood filled with pine trees and tree forts, streetlights and "The Beverly Hillbillies," and a rampart of factories that surrounded everything. It's a meditation on growing older, where "the wet lifejackets of loss hang useless on shore." We journey with Daniels from Detroit and Warren, Michigan, to Pittsburgh and Florida and to tiny villages in France, all the while contemplating what it means to be fully human across time and place, past and present. "I've been dreaming of symmetry my whole life, so I imagine it in many places of imbalance," Daniels writes in just one of many moments of beautiful insight, honesty, and grace. And ultimately symmetry.

—LORI JAKIELA
author of *All Skate: True Stories from Middle Life*

An
Ignorance
of Trees

a memoir in essays

Jim Daniels

CORNERSTONE PRESS
UNIVERSITY OF WISCONSIN-STEVENS POINT

Cornerstone Press, Stevens Point, Wisconsin 54481
Copyright © 2025 Jim Daniels
www.uwsp.edu/cornerstone

Printed in the United States of America.

Library of Congress Control Number: 2025940338
ISBN: 978-1-960329-91-2

Cover art: "Sol Invictus" © 2007 Anselm Kiefer. Used by permission of the artist.

This is a work of nonfiction. All of the events in this book are true to the best of the author's memories. Some names and identifying features have been changed to protect the identity of certain parties. The author in no way represents any company, corporation, or brand, mentioned herein. The views expressed in this book are solely those of the author.

Cornerstone Press titles are produced in courses and internships offered by the Department of English at the University of Wisconsin–Stevens Point.

DIRECTOR & PUBLISHER
Dr. Ross K. Tangedal

EXECUTIVE EDITORS
Jeff Snowbarger, Freesia McKee

EDITORIAL DIRECTOR
Brett Hill

SENIOR EDITOR
Ellie Atkinson

PRESS STAFF
Paige Biever, Reilly Crous, Karlie Harpold, Kim Janesch, Sam Zajkowski, Allison Lange, Sophie McPherson, Ava Willett, Madison Schultz, Autumn Vine

ALSO BY JIM DANIELS:

POETRY

Comment Card

The Human Engine at Dawn

Gun/Shy

The Middle Ages

Street Calligraphy

Rowing Inland

Apology to the Moon

Birth Marks

All of the Above

Having a Little Talk with Capital P Poetry

From Milltown to Malltown

In Line for the Exterminator

Revolt of the Crash-Test Dummies

Now Showing

Street

Show and Tell: New and Selected Poems

Digger's Blues

Night with Drive-by Shooting Stars

Greatest Hits

Black Vinyl, Red Vinyl

Blue Jesus

Blessing the House

Niagara Falls

M-80

Hacking It

Punching Out

Digger's Territory

ESSAYS

AUTHOR'S NOTE

The events in these essays are portrayed to the best of my imperfect memory. I've tried to recreate experiences, places, and people from various times in the past, some of them quite distant, so that imperfection might be more apparent at some times than others. Some names and identifying details have been changed to protect the privacy of the people involved.

—Jim Daniels

WINDBLOWN:
RE-CAPTURING THE FLAG

He made us each a flag. We kept them there, rolled up and leaned into a corner, and when our grandfather unlocked the cottage door, my brothers and I each grabbed ours and charged outside, unfurling our cramped voices from the long drive in the back seat of whatever fixer-upper he'd recently fixed up.

Someone got the black-and-yellow checkered flag, someone got the green canvas flag, and someone got the off-white thick starchy piece of burlap. He nailed them each to poles—a random piece of floorboard molding for the checkered flag, a dowel rod for the green, and for the white one, which we never associated with weakness or surrender, a piece of bamboo.

The tiny cottage—the size of a one-car garage—wasn't quite on Lake Huron. It sat a quarter-mile inland down a dirt road they oiled in summer to keep the dust down, past the nicer cottages on the water to the public access point. But we were close enough to feel the breeze up from the small, rocky patch of sand we grew to call Ankle Beach behind his back as he lost his hearing and we lost interest. Ankle Beach, because he could not swim and thus could not let us swim. Even though by then we could swim. We were only allowed to stick our toes in and numb them. We could skip stones till our arms were sore.

We could sit and study the horizon for Great Lakes freighters passing silently and dignified in the distance.

I believe the freighters were mirages for the kind of life my grandfather once imagined. He had wanted to see the world, or at least beyond Canada. We didn't know then. We loved him. He had made us flags.

I HAVE BEGUN TO DISTRUST the American flag. A lot of people might distrust me for saying that. The showy, extravagant display of the American flag—or, more accurately, flags plural—is it becoming a dog whistle for fascism?

Oh, don't go overboard, somebody might say. Or, throw him overboard, someone else might say. In either case, I might end up in the water, though despite not being able to wade out from Ankle Beach, I still learned to swim.

The wet lifejackets of loss hang useless on shore.

SINCE NOBODY CHANGES anybody else's minds these days—these stripes don't bleed, right?—I won't delve into the shark-infested political waters except to stick my toe in and say I believed in American democracy so much that I took it for granted. You can't have too many/fly too many American flags anymore. You never know when you'll have to stuff one in somebody's mouth to silence them.

MY GRANDFATHER LOST two children before they were out of school, leaving my lonely father to carry the family flag. I can't carbon-date the non-finishing of the cottage, but given the family silence, I've been forced to become fairly proficient with my guess-ometer. The silver insulation between the studs flashed at us day and night, shrinking us, distorting us like funhouse mirrors.

We, his only grandchildren, woke him up out of his decades-long stupor into restless sleepwalking. He never had much, and what he loved most had been taken away from him.

When he was a boy, my grandfather's brother choked on a chicken bone one Sunday morning while his father was cleaning out his bar after a typical Saturday night in Belgian Detroit. I never learned where my grandfather was when this happened because I never learned this happened at all until after he was dead. And I never learned about my phantom aunt and uncle from him either. My father finally broke the silence when I was in college after I had run into someone who'd been a friend of my dead uncle. Jack was his name. Katherine was my aunt's name.

Silence was what we had. The language we spoke. The language of sitting on shore looking for freighters took a lot of patience to learn.

STAY WITH ME HERE on Ankle Beach and imagine all of us—however you define us, and that in itself is a contentious issue, a bone of contention to choke on—sitting on shore in silence and watching a freighter slowly drift across the horizon. And all we can do is sigh.

LIFE IS FULL OF MIRAGES, of course, but maybe this heat is cooking up more of them. Resulting in injuries that come from rubbing our eyes too fiercely.

THE FLAGS GAVE US SOMETHING to carry and run with. Not fight wars over. Not with my brothers. Oh, we fought like brothers fought, but it was never about sticking our flags in the ground and marking our territory.

Away from the beach, nobody fenced off their tiny cottages. We could run forever with those flags, and we did. Finally bending over to huff and puff and laugh at each other.

We kept them rolled up in the bedroom next to the autographed picture of the cowboy singer and actor Roy Rogers on the wall. It wasn't real but torn from an old magazine. How old, we never knew—Rogers' career spanned from the 30s up to around 1990, so I wonder if my father and his brother had looked at this same picture as boys.

When we were at the cottage for weekends with my grandfather, real wasn't so important. He wore his stained green work pants from when he had a job fixing engines. He kept three broken lawnmowers at the cottage. He was a lawnmower Houdini, switching parts out till one of them started up and allowed him to cut the tough overgrown weeds. No grass. Just stiff weeds. No fences, no lawns, and no running water. What more could a young boy need?

Why did he never finish the insides of the cottage, leaving it shell-like, echoey? Though we never heard the sound of the sea inside that shell, when the wind was right and the waves were kicking up off the lake, we would faintly hear the crashing in our jumbled boy-dreams as we slept on the two soft, cramped mattresses—so soft those waves could have been tumbling us through those breezy walls.

We might have yelled when we ran with the flags, but it was not words. Just boy-sounds. We didn't capture anyone's flag, though I admit we had become attached to our own and were somewhat possessive. None of us knows what became of them. Perhaps they were deliberately drowned by stars and stripes.

We were a triumvirate of flags over the weeds, shiny grass stains on our knees from falling, then getting up. We, a trinity, horsemen without horses, warriors without war. Oh, even now on rare quiet days, I hear our rumbling hooves and laughter.

SWING SET:
THE GIANT'S FOOTSTEPS

After the end of World War II, as Americans returned to a life of prosperity, families moved to the suburbs, and everyone wanted the best outdoor swing sets in their own backyard. The home swing set was born...Early 20th century playgrounds were made of steel, and this caused many injuries and inspired later play sets to be constructed of softer materials like plastic and wood.

transcendence: *existence or experience beyond the normal or physical level: "the possibility of spiritual transcendence in the modern world."*

On the edge of Detroit, in our backyard in Warren, Michigan, the third-largest city in the state despite having no downtown, we had no trees, no swimming pool, no trampoline, no statuary, and very little grass. What we had was a swing set.

When you look at pictures of swing sets online, they're always in some ultra-lush green idyllic yard. Something Cain and Abel might've played on before they had a fight over who got the good swing. Our backyard was clearly post-fight. The weeds we called grass quickly turned into dirt ruts beneath the two swings, worn away by pushing off before we were high enough to start pumping.

THE FACTORIES WERE our city centers, rimmed with strip malls and tract housing. Three major auto factories stood within two square miles of our home. My father worked at the Ford Sterling Axle Plant at Seventeen Mile and Mound Roads. We navigated by mile roads, from Six Mile Road out to 38 Mile Road. Those, along with the slightly more creatively named crossroads, created a grid of square-mile boxes filled with the tiny boxes of our identical houses surrounding the much larger boxes, the boxes of industry, the car factories. Our neighborhood of factory workers went up in the Fifties.

One of those houses was ours, and I was one of five children in that tiny three-bedroom ranch, along with my parents and grandmother. One Saturday when he was off work, my father erected the swing set in our backyard while we stood watching at a distance as instructed.

Backyard swing sets came without anything to anchor them into the ground. If you just set it up in the yard, it was likely to tip over, particularly if you had five kids rocking it back and forth. My father quickly realized the problem and tried to solve it the way he tried to solve most problems: with a bag of cement. He dug out circles around the swing set's four feet and filled them with concrete, thinking they'd hold it down to earth. Nice try, Dad.

The swing set didn't change everything, but it changed a lot.

Human blood, which also contains water and iron, has a smell similar to rust.

OUR SWING SET HAD two flat metal swings hanging on chains that quickly rusted. I remember them as always rusty, our hands orange-brown from gripping them as we pumped the swings high. Higher. The comfort of the gritty rust in my hands. A safety feature for the soul. Visible, tactile, with a metallic smell that gave a tangible connection to earth, even as we flew.

It also had a "glide ride," a heavy metal contraption that two kids could ride on, facing each other on connected metal seats with matching handles and footrests. By pumping the handles, you could get the thing swinging back and forth, more horizontal than vertical due to the limited length of its metal arms attached to the cross bar above.

None of us wanted to look at each other that close up. None of us wanted to be stuck on that small track going back and forth. The glide ride had no maneuverability, or even the illusion of it, particularly as it rusted.

Not only were we limited by its low arc even when we were pumping hardest, but the pumpers and footrests were welded in place. Once we reached a certain height, when we put our feet down, our knees ended up around our shoulders, which gave us no leverage to pump and left us hunched over like some of the old factory workers I ended up working with. We had the rest of our lives to bend down into human question marks. And why bother with the glide ride when we had swings? Despite its limited mythology of smooth grace, it rusted out so badly that our father unscrewed it from the cross bar and threw it out. Cain had slain Abel by then, so what was the point?

WHILE I ONLY LATER LEARNED of the concept of the "golden handcuffs" our fathers wore, the glide ride was like a simulator. Working in the factory provided a decent middle-class income. You could afford to buy a house, raise kids, and get a new car every so often—a big car, so all the kids fit. Yet an assembly-line worker had no upward mobility—like the glide ride, there was a very limited range of motion, no escape route that wasn't risking a financial plunge into a minimum-wage job. The glide ride lifted us up a little in each direction but never got us anywhere. It mimicked the repetitive, mechanical work of the assembly line where you couldn't stray far. The rigid assembly line relentlessly kept on moving, and you had to be there to attach your flanges, your brake cables, your axle housings—somebody was standing right next to you waiting to attach something else. Machines controlled the pace of our work. Regardless of gender, factory workers had a glass ceiling—or maybe a rust ceiling, entirely too visible.

When I worked in the Ford Axle Plant in the late 70s, like my father and my younger brother, all of the various jobs I had were equally repetitive and mechanical. Put in a part, push two buttons, take it out, put in a part, push two buttons, take it out. At the end of the shift, I got off the glide ride and went home. No physical evidence of the work I did—it had been carried off by hi-los into the bowels of the factory to be loaded on train cars and shipped off to some assembly plant.

IN ADDITION TO THE GLIDE ride and swings, we used every inch of that swing set, finding new uses as we grew. The crossbar that held the two angled poles together was ideal for swinging upside down by our legs to make ourselves dizzy, and we also climbed onto it to allow us to reach over and swing from the thick crossbar across the top of the set. We did chin-ups on that bar. We had kick fights to knock each other down, imagining a pit full of snakes or sharks or alligators beneath us. Imagining ourselves as Great Apes. Imagining our lives at risk. Imagining.

The concept and meaning of risk changed as we aged. As kids, the risk of our fathers losing their factory jobs never occurred to us. The notion that anything as large and permanent as the factories would disappear seemed ludicrous. We drove by their gray massive rectangular boxes on the way to and from almost everything. They existed as permanent fixtures in our lives, as permanent as the church—and as boring and repetitious, ultimately—and we worshiped and resented them as the source for everything we had. To us, they were equally as mysterious and scary as churches—even more so, since, unlike with church, we never entered those factories. Until we did, as employees. If somebody had to work overtime on a Sunday, work took priority over church. As was often said, "Jesus doesn't pay the bills."

Priorities were a mixed bag for every person and every family, but it was a bag inside a large box we all shared called The Factory. Every aspect of our lives took place in the context—in the giant shadow—of The Factory, whether it was Ford's, Chrysler's, or GM's. Our swing set was situated in that context, much more than I realized at the time. I know the parallels I'm trying to draw here are often not parallel at all, but crossed lines, Xs of conflict—but in some ways, at some points, they all seem true.

IF YOU'VE EVER SWUNG on a real swing—I'm thinking of the large ones with rubber saddle seats, something black, durable, and flexible for your ass to drop into—then you know the goal was to get as high as you could, then jump off and land without breaking a leg. Exhilaration and fear. The same emotions that drive race car drivers, mountain climbers, and perhaps bank robbers.

When I use "real," I am referring back to the days before playground equipment was designed for three-year-olds—safety swings that only swung as high as the height of your average adult, and slides at that same height. Hardly worth the effort to climb the four steps. Not even a climb, really, the slope so gradual that my own children took to walking up them—a low, plastic incline that made the slide so slow that the kids often had to scoot their butts and push their hands off the edges just to make it to the bottom.

One of the things contemporary playground designers (and/or the insurance companies) don't seem to understand is that play benefits from a little fear. How many kids on playgrounds today look bored out of their minds? The ones that seem to be having fun are those kids chasing each other—motivated by the excitement of catching someone, and the fear of being caught. They need no equipment for this. I believe this is a game called Tag.

I PROBABLY SHOULDN'T BE idealizing our rusty swings when often the metal seat would ricochet off somebody's head in its wild dance once you jumped. I acknowledge sounding like an old fogey nostalgic for broken limbs, even though I want to sound like someone with a longing for risk and individuality—the glorious seconds of flying, free of the chains, the exhilaration of possibility, even if it meant injury, in a world where even for us as children, it felt like nothing would ever change. I'm trying to make sense of those brief seconds in the air after jumping off as the happiest moments of my childhood.

Our houses were identical, and we rarely left them. While I suspect some families went on vacation during the summer, in our neighborhood it was a rarity. Men like my father used vacation time to work on their homes. Over the course of several years, he built a bedroom in the basement so that the four boys would no longer be squeezed into the one tiny room upstairs clogged with two bunk beds. My older brothers were teenagers when he finally finished it—well, he admits that he never really quite finished it, but it was good enough for them to move in down there. The swing set came down shortly afterward.

On our streets, I could walk into any house and find the bathroom. I knew what kind of car everyone drove, how many kids in each house, and all their names. We all knew where our fathers worked: The Factory. While it was one of the Big Three, or one of the hundreds of small tool and die and manufacturing plants (baby factories surrounding momma and papa factories), our fathers wore similar coveralls and carried identical lunch pails, thrown in the car every morning, just like we carried our brown paper bags to school with our initials on them to distinguish them from all the other bag lunches.

I WORKED IN THE FACTORY right before the bottom fell out of the American auto industry, back when one of the few ways to distinguish yourself from the thousands of workers doing nearly identical jobs was to engage in workplace sabotage. Ideally, with some payoff that involved avoiding doing our jobs correctly, since that consisted of working exactly like a machine worked. It was a natural impulse to literally throw a wrench in the machinery.

For example, at the Sterling Axle Plant, we had, for a surprisingly long time until it was finally exposed, a secret "punch card club." Each job had a production number—how many parts you were expected to make per shift (mine was 800). Once you achieved this magic number, you could disappear for the rest of your shift. On the midnight shift, disappearance was taken literally, with workers sneaking out of the plant halfway through their shifts to drink or sleep while still on Ford's dime. Making production was accomplished through a variety of shady methods, including "stealing" axle parts made by the two other shifts and splashing "midnight-blue" paint on them and driving pallets of them on hi-los to the midnight-shift storage area; through what we called "jacking off" (physically manipulating) the automatic counters on machines; through retrieving scrapped parts, ripping off the red "Rejected" tags and labeling them with the green "O.K." tag. One way or another, workers were able to give the illusion they'd made their production number for the shift.

The next trick was getting out of the plant. At that time, our plastic photo ID cards had computer holes cut in them so that they could also be used to punch in and out at the time clocks. Some genius realized that you could cut the plastic out of, say, a bleach bottle, punch the same holes in it, and use it as a spare ID card. You'd give this card to some guy, along with a dollar, and he'd punch you, and dozens of other workers, out at the time clock at the end of the shift while you were long gone.

Left to their own devices, our fathers *could* build a better mousetrap. A better swing set. Walking out of the factory during the middle of a shift was as exhilarating as jumping off a swing into the midnight air.

Though I never saw my father sit on a swing. He preferred a good, firm chair like his La-Z-Boy, manufactured down the road in Monroe, Michigan. His pushing off the floor to tilt the chair backward toward the horizontal was a counterpoint to our push, pumping our arms and legs on the swing toward the vertical.

THE ABSENCE OF A slide on our swing set is a mystery. Most swing sets came with slides. You climbed up, you slid down. Why didn't ours have one? Perhaps the narrow dimensions of our yard did not allow it. Perhaps our father could not afford it. Perhaps he felt like life was all downhill as it was, and felt no need to emphasize that to us when we were still kids.

We had to go to public playgrounds to find a slide. The ones in our area were all constructed on cement slabs. Swings, monkey bars, merry-go-rounds, and slides, all anchored in that concrete sea. Our closest playground was at Neigebaur Elementary, about a mile or so away. To walk to it required us to cross one of those reckless mile roads congested with mad cars rushing to and from the factories. Thus, it was off limits, and the backyard swing set was decreed less dangerous in all respects until we reached a certain age where it was deemed safe enough for us to cross those streets alone.

We could safely get to that playground in order to risk our lives. Real slides were scary—just climbing up the metal steps could be daunting. You could easily trip and fall off those steps, particularly if the person behind you was pulling on your leg, telling you to hurry up.

Daunting, yet magnificent. Skyscraper slides. Steep and treacherous, with a concrete landing awaiting at the bottom.

In summer, in order to make them even slicker, we'd throw dry sand down the slide in front of us, and if you dared to wear shorts, you had the added risk of burning your legs on their reflected metal heat. In the winter, you could throw snow on the slide, which also made them quicker. We tried to sabotage any safety with the goal of scaring ourselves even more.

OUR FACTORY, like many others, had a sign at the entrance that listed how many days since the last work-loss accident. Based on my observations, it never made it into the triple figures. I would guess if the cement playground had a similar sign, that number would be similarly restricted. I chipped a permanent tooth on one of those monkey bars.

Numbers. Restrictions. Cement landing pads. Control. No control. Emergency chutes on airplanes. Don't inflate your life vest until you land in the water or else you won't fit down the chute. Learn to swim. At least dog-paddle.

BUT WE had swings.

The official playgrounds took theirs down in winter. But on the Daniels' swing set, the swings remained. The rough winters of the 60s may have contributed to the rusting, but jumping off a swing onto untrampled snow was truly magical, and maybe even safer than in summer. Deep, soft snow. The crisp whump and sprawl of the landing, washing your own face in snow in ritual cleansing. Snow pushed its way up your pants, down the neck of your jacket, inside your hat and mittens. Life was deliciously cold when landing in fresh snow.

PUSHING OFF WAS the most useful skill we took away from our years of swinging. The simplicity of a swing is that it has no engine. Just the human engine. In order to get a start, to launch, you need thrust, gravity, feet boosters—I don't know the technical terms. You need a firm base on the ground to push off from. A strong push backward with two feet to get a good start on swinging height. Then, you begin to pump your legs and arms in synchronous motion—loose, natural, as if you were born with the instinct to swing. You pull your torso forward, then lean back. *High. Higher.* Until on the backswing, your head rises higher than the crossbar. Your stomach flippity-flops in the millisecond of cresting, then back down, and you feel the moment coming in the next swoop upward and you release the chains at the highest point and you are flying, momentum carrying you even higher before the inevitable plunge to earth, and you tumble forward through the weeds, unhurt and inexplicably laughing, exhilarated. Maybe you even get the giddy hiccups of laughter. You could be alone in the backyard, but the laughter is contagious nevertheless. You infect yourself with it.

Making a mud pie…consists of creating a mixture of water and soil and playing or pretending to make food or a pie. Mud pies are not meant to be eaten.

Mud pie argument: The argument against the labor theory of value pointing out that mud pies that take an immense amount of labor still have little to no value.

WE ERODED OUR OWN launch pads beneath us. The push-off zones quickly turned into mud puddles in any kind of rain. But part of our joy involved embracing the mud splattering onto us. Maybe we looked something like our greasy fathers when they finished a shift.

Getting muddy was one thing. But making mud pies was something entirely different. We never made mud pies. I'm convinced it's some sanitized upper-class notion of how poor kids play to go along with the idealized images of the swing set on the perfectly groomed lawn. How cute. To us, it seemed stupid to pretend mud was food—our fathers worked hard so we would not have to eat mud. What was the point, the payoff? The risk? Our lives didn't allow for the luxury of that kind of imagination. Where was the possibility of transcendence? Yes, transcendence. Not wallowing. Not pretending mud is not mud.

IF OUR ANONYMOUS streets were part of a maze, they would all lead to those factories and offer no exit. How early on were we conscious of our futures being mapped out in this way? I'm not sure. We knew our father worked in one of them. We knew he rarely came home before dark. We knew he didn't want to play with us when he got home.

Or, maybe our lives were more funnel than maze—the inevitability of us working in those factories, gravity pulling us down into them. But we might be able to at least afford one of those box houses for ourselves someday. And maybe our kids could make mud pies and live happily ever after.

YES, THESE DAYS, that maze has more dead ends and less inevitability than ever, due to the ongoing process of deindustrialization, robots, the impact of foreign competition, and, I admit, some residual quality-control issues from back in the glory days when we couldn't get the cars out onto the lots fast enough. Or, maybe it's not a maze. In the Rust Belt, we still wear that belt, despite its imperfections. Or, maybe it's not a belt. But that smell of rust is still in our blood—not visible to the naked eye, but something coursing through us. An attitude that appreciates the flight as much as the fall. That mythologizes it due to the inability to find real swings anymore. The attitude that got me in trouble in my forty years of university teaching, struggling with "Imposter Syndrome."

Despite the diminishing factory jobs, the Ford Sterling Axle Plant still employs approximately 2,250 people to make those mudpies on its 171 acres. It opened in 1956, the year I was born. The axle plant and I will celebrate our 68th birthdays this year. It's been 46 years since I set foot in that factory, and at least a couple dozen since I swung on tiny swings with my own children on a spongy safety surface of ground-up car tires, unable to pump any higher than my own height. Maybe 56 since I swung on the swing set back in Warren.

THE CEMENT GLOBES my father installed around the swing set's feet to hold it down were like cement shoes for us to match his own. As if we were holding *ourselves* down. Was that cement made of crushed-up dollar bills and coins, pressed together into a middle-class life, high enough, but no higher?

But the cement around the four legs did not deter us. As we grew bigger and got stronger, we realized that two kids swinging hard in sync could rock the rear legs out of the ground with their forward momentum, cement and all, and when we swung back, the front legs would pop up. One kid alone could not make this happen, but together...together anything was possible. Coordination, cooperation, solidarity, moving forward (and backward) as one.

When the cement-globed legs returned to earth, the ground shook with the thick thud. We were taking control. Imposing our will on that metal structure. And as we got bigger and stronger yet, we could even get the legs to hop out of their holes and move forward, inch by inch. We called them Giant Steps when we got the swing set rocking forward. Fee-Fi-Fo-Fum.

None of us ever broke a bone in the mucky weeds of our backyard. We learned how to land, just like we learned how to push off. Sometimes we got the wind knocked out of us.

I CAN STILL IMAGINE those orange rust stains on my hands, the rust that did in the swing set finally, the crossbar dangerously eroding. To be honest, I don't remember how my father got rid of it. We must've been big enough to help him then, but I don't think we did.

We didn't move mountains, or even hills. We moved a small swing set a few feet forward in an anonymous backyard. Baby steps, really, but for us, growing up in that land of cement and steel, we briefly felt like giants rocking the earth, and we felt like birds when we let go and flew into the air. Giants and birds. What more could anyone ask for in a small yard of a three-bedroom tract house on the edge of Detroit, in sight of the factory down the road puffing its impatient heavy breath, waiting to swallow us?

AN IGNORANCE OF TREES

...turning all the forests of the world into rectangles.
—Richard Powers, *The Overstory*

...all you can about animals as persons.
the names of trees and flowers and weeds.
names of stars, and the movements of the planets
and the moon.

—Gary Snyder, "What You Should Know to Be a Poet"

NAMING NAMES

I know the names of more cars than trees. It's not something I'm proud of—it's a simple fact. Identifying cars was an important skill in our neighborhood in Warren on the edge of Detroit. It meant you were informed—cool, hip to what mattered. Intelligence in school was not particularly valued, since our fate was in plain sight around us: we either surrounded the auto plants or they surrounded us, depending on your perspective.

The names of cars—make, model, year. The names of parts and how to fix your car with them, back when doing that was more muscular and less computerized. What kind of car you drove makes a statement, and while this is true for everyone, everywhere, it seems particularly true in Detroit, where we build them. Hilarious to imagine anyone in our neighborhood saying, "Hey, did you see that beautiful oak tree over on Eight Mile Road?" If I remembered seeing any trees along Eight Mile Road, they were green blurs in the median strip of that eight-lane road, an expressway with red lights. Something about speed—and being in a car, metal and glass serving as a barricade between you and whatever nature was out there—made trees inconsequential. Unless you happened to slide off the road on black ice and wrap your car around one.

We had no streets named Maple, Oak, or Birch. The numbered mile roads, from Eight Mile to Fourteen Mile, helped create the grid that cornered Warren off into squares. Cement. Parking lots. Factories. Freeways. The Motor City, and for a time, they couldn't build enough roads for all the cars. They covered up the streetcar tracks. Mass transit was a bug stomped out by the Big Three.

LANDSCAPE ARCHITECTURE

We had no statues or swimming pools or trampolines in our yards. And very little grass. Mostly dandelions and clover and brown spots from dogs and their shit. Except for the two legendary lawns on the block, tended to by Mr. B. and Crazy Eddie, who manicured their grass with fanatical zeal in some mad competition only they cared about. Lawnmowers, edgers, trimmers, toxic fertilizers. These guys actually watered driveways and sidewalks, as if they'd shrivel up and crumble otherwise. What drove them toward that absurd perfection? Neither of them had sons; a total of three daughters between them, and maybe that fed a certain compensatory grudge, a peculiar meanness that set them even further apart from their neighbors. Crazy Eddie was our prototypical ball snatcher. Why does every neighborhood have one, and who assigns them these roles? If a ball landed on his grass, it instantly disappeared, zapped into some other universe, which turned out to be a laundry basket in his basement. He legendarily massacred the pigeons that lonely

Mrs. Parsons used to feed next door because they were shitting on his roof. He either shot them or poisoned them with lawn fertilizer, depending on who's telling the story.

When some boys, who I happened to know, burned "FUCK YO" into Crazy Eddie's lawn with salt one summer night (they ran out of salt for the U), that too became legendary. We hit him where he was most vulnerable. It was only in such a magnificent lawn that those letters stood out as much as they did—as if they were painted on, though the salt did greater and more permanent damage than any paint could.

Mrs. Parsons had a tall cinderblock wall built between their houses—the Berlin Wall of Bach Street. We believed that good fences meant good fences, that any problem could be solved with cement and bricks.

Despite cement walls, we could still see our futures clearly because we had no hills to block the view, and few trees of any size, and none thicker than a human wrist. Visiting relatives from the Old Country or from Down South (where the factories mined for workers) often commented on the flatness, expecting there to be an airport nearby. The only hills we had consisted of seasonal snow plowed into messy mountains on the edges of parking lots, hills that turned black with soot before finally melting, despite nearby cities named Sterling Heights, Rochester Hills, Bloomfield Hills—heights and hills, just words thrown in for imaginary status in the suburban grid. The flatness allowed easy steamrolling over the old farmland with concrete and blacktop—out, then further out, away from the polluted Detroit River, leaving parts of Detroit with block after block of abandoned houses, then rubble.

LET THE MYSTERY BE

Our house became legendary in its own way. No one will ever know why the trees in our yard died, but they always did, one at a time, all planted stubbornly in the same place. I want to say what kinds of trees, but they didn't last long enough to establish identity—or for me to remember how many there were. The developer planted one in each front yard down Rome Street, and they met with spotty success as well. Just not quite as bad as ours: "Your dad's not gonna try and plant another tree there, is he?" The answer was yes. Just when we thought he'd given up the fight, he'd show up some miscellaneous Saturday with yet another tree from Frank's Nursery hanging out of the trunk with a red flag tied to it, as required by law. Frank's, the only place to buy a tree this side of the Ford plant where he worked.

There should be a law that you can't bring anything home that doesn't fit in your trunk, red tag or no. If you can't slam the trunk closed on it, leave it behind. While multiple bags of cement fit nicely in a trunk, heavy enough to noticeably lower the rear end of a car, nothing that extends outward should be tolerated.

My father should have known better than to try again—to re-tie the red flag—given his inclination to cut things down to reasonable size—our size—in our overly reasonable neighborhood. He'd ceremoniously get out his shovel and gloves and get to work. Never a fan of subtlety, if my father ever talked to a tree, he'd have said, "Grow, damn it!" He didn't want any help. He'd kill it himself, thank you.

I remember what may have been dead oak leaves holding onto one tree long after its demise, until my father finally dug it up and sawed it into a few pieces to fit inside a trash can.

And I remember standing at a distance—the way we always stood around our father—watching him unswathe a root ball, cutting away the burlap, trying to pry the roots loose from their tight round tangle and plant a tree in the perfect symmetrical place for one, centered in the long thin rectangle of lawn between the sidewalk and the street, parallel with the round sewer drain scooped out of the curb in a swirl on the concrete street.

We were not a symmetrical family. Five kids within eight years, and that included the ghost kid my mother lost in between me and my younger brother. My grandmother came to live with us, and she shared a room with my sister for fifteen years before becoming a ghost herself. Privacy was a myth. Perhaps the lack of privacy killed those trees.

A PINE IS A PINE IS A PINE

Frank's Nursery was also where we got our Christmas tree every year—a balsam fir, because our mother loved the smell, and the needles were softer than the spiky Scotch pines. The tree was already dead, so all it needed to do was hold its needles for a week or two. Frank was like Santa Claus in that there was more than one Frank, and he could be in different places at the same time. It was said that he kept his green thumb in a safe.

Those were the only trees I could name—Scotch pines and balsam firs. While I may have heard of the stately blue spruce or Douglas fir, they seemed to be in the price range of neighborhoods further north of Detroit—the Heights or Hills. We knew Christmas trees. We divided trees into pines and not pines. Evergreens that stayed ever-green, and trees that lost their leaves in fall. We used pine and evergreen interchangeably. Pine trees had needles, not leaves. We knew the sharp smell. We knew what our father knew. That was the extent of our meager knowledge.

Bushes were evergreens too. We just called them bushes. Except for picker bushes, which we just called pickers, and were strategically located around the corner lots to try and keep us from cutting the angle. I think our childhoods consisted mainly of trying to make shortcuts, imperfect footpaths in our world of 90-degree concrete angles forming boxes. We slanted across to make our wandering marks, as if bowling endless spares, knowing there were no strikes in our futures. Or, if there were, we weren't winning them.

ROBIN IN THE HOOD

Our house, identical to every house on the block, was so small that my father tore down a closet so we could all sit in the living room. We were a family of hooks, not hangers.

His oldest friend Pat Callahan came over to help. Pat was still drinking then, which might explain why they got out my father's bow and shot arrows into the drywall of the empty closet before tearing it down. They may have drawn a wobbly target on it first. They were both wobbly with laughter by the time they got out the sledgehammer and shooed us out of the room—or our mother did—due to various dangers. They ended up covering themselves in white plaster, a kind of ghostly city camouflage, but no one got hurt. When that dust cleared, my father put his La-Z-Boy knockoff there, where it remained for the next forty years.

The bow and arrow's existence, in a quiver on a hook in our basement, was completely incongruous. My father, a boy from Detroit, owned a real-live bow and quiver? We sometimes gently touched the soft feathers of his dozen arrows and their sharp points while he was at work in the factory. Where, when, and what had he imagined shooting with that bow? Not a closet, I imagine. He never said. Not a big talker, that guy.

I keep trying to connect the bow and arrows with the dead trees, to justify an equal sign. Perhaps that link was buried in the rubble of that closet. The equal sign? Maybe it's the two paved tracks up the driveway for car wheels with a stretch of weeds in between.

PLACE UP NORTH

When I was in college, my father succumbed to the opium dream of Detroit auto workers and bought a hunting cabin up north in Newaygo, downstream from Pat Callahan's father's cottage. He'd gone deer hunting there a couple of times with Pat, and the sharp smell of those pine trees went to his head. These guys were not hunters in any serious way. It was just another myth they bought into for a time to give them something to think about during their long hours at the factory.

One fateful year, wandering apart from each other in the woods, the mighty hunters both shot a doe, though they only had gotten one doe permit from the state lottery. After meeting up to tell each other the good news and realizing the bad news, they decided to clean one deer and bury the other one. Pat made my father clean the deer while he threw up. I think he'd stopped drinking by then, so it wasn't that kind of sick. They were city kids, and cutting open an animal was something they somehow hadn't anticipated. No one ate the deer heart.

During those trips, my father had taken to being in the untamed woods bordering the Bigelow Stream. I'm not sure what it offered him—perhaps the novelty of peace and pine and rushing water. But I knew what it took him away from—noisy traffic, city, factory—his completely controlled world back home. And our house crammed with five kids and his mother-in-law. When Pat told him a neighbor was selling his place on the stream—a tiny ancient camping trailer with a flimsy wooden screened-in porch built onto it—the price was right (low, even for a ramshackle wreck with its tiny trailer toilet and jimmy-rigged septic system). My father bought it without his characteristic hesitation when it came to spending any significant sum of money. The only exception being, of course, his car purchases, since it helped the company, and the employee discount was attractive.

He was forty-seven years old then, and a three-and-a-half-hour drive was not a big deal, particularly with my mother along to help. But as he got older, it became a less and less attractive prospect. The long drive stretched longer as my mother began to lose her vision and her strength, and the rodent-infested, damp trailer with its many leaks and mold became too much to manage.

But, oh, when you first stepped out of the car down in that valley, the sweet, sharp smell of pine hit you. The simple abundance was intoxicating—endless pine trees swaying their welcome. It woke you up, that smell, like—like the opposite of a ton of bricks, and that's what we were used to back in Warren and its vast flat "farmland" of three-bedroom ranches.

In Newaygo, he didn't have to plant trees. He had to cut them down—he didn't have to do this either, but he thought he did. He took great pleasure in it. They were always somehow encroaching. Give that man a chainsaw and get out of the way! It gave him a power he didn't have in daily life—cutting, clearing, happy as a kid with a Tonka truck digging in a sandbox.

One day he couldn't help himself and took a piece of Newaygo home with him, digging up a pine sapling near a rotting corner of the trailer and driving it back down to Warren to plant in our front yard. He picked a new spot, closer to the house, on the bigger quadrant of lawn bisected by the sidewalk up to the porch. The five of us were mostly grown then—working, in college, or finishing up high school—and not at risk of trampling it. Nobody played games out front anymore—no red light/green light, no pom-pom tackle, no red rover, no kill-the-guy-with-the-ball (our favorite). I keep a faded flash photo of me in the yard one night at Christmas: a young man, home on break from college, crouched next to a small snowman he built next to the then-tiny pine tree. I don't know who took the picture. Maybe the streetlight.

The tree thrived. On Google Maps, it now dominates the streetside photo, the proportion completely out of whack—that tree dwarfs the house. The fallen needles lie in a brown circle on the ground around it that might remind a few boys of a Christmas tree fort they once built.

I have to search on Google now, since my parents sold the house back in 2001 and downsized into a condo. My father at 95 doesn't drive much anymore, and even ten miles further down Ryan Road to the old house is too far for him. Sometimes when he's restless, I drive him through the old neighborhood and we idle in front of the house to marvel at that tree. I wait till he tells me we can move on. I think part of him would like to get the chainsaw out and cut down that big overgrown sucker. Put it in its place.

THE CHRISTMAS TREE FORT

One year, on garbage night in early January, my brothers and I had this bright idea. Most of our bright ideas involved trying to distinguish ourselves in one way or another—positive or negative didn't seem to matter much. Just to stick out briefly from our anonymity was enough. Back then, everyone got real Christmas trees, and as we took ours to the curb, we noticed all the neighbors' trees set out next to their trash cans. We dragged them all—I'm guessing a couple of dozen—into our snow-covered front yard and stacked them up into a squarish structure we called a fort. Needles rained everywhere from all those dry trees. They poked through our gloves and hats and heavy jeans, but we didn't care—the shelter of those trees kept us from numbing up in the cold. We spent hours inside the fort, waiting for an attack, I suppose. The neighbors must have gotten a kick out of driving past, thinking about my poor father, who was incapable of keeping a tree alive, being burdened with all those dead ones. My father himself seemed to barely notice when he pulled up the driveway in the dark after another twelve-hour shift. I don't remember him ever commenting on it.

What I remember most about the fort is, again, the intense pine smell. Later, when I began smoking, the cool sting of menthol cigarettes reminded me of that fort. The sting in our nostrils, waking up our senses, imagining we were in a forest and someone or something might attack us. The sap stuck on our hands or gloves. Something primitive had drifted, then hovered over our plain regimented lives of sidewalks and drive-ways shoveled into neat squares and rectangles. Our unruly fort stuck out like a bombing target or a call for help from passing police helicopters or the occasional errant small plane headed for Detroit City Airport.

I can't remember how long the tree fort stood, but I do remember that when we finally dragged the brown, skeletal trees into a pile by the curb, the snow had mostly melted and the grass, such as it was, had begun to green. The trashmen took them away, crunching them one by one in the loud giant maw of their truck. What remained behind? A misshapen square of dead grass sprinkled with needles, like the map of some foreign country we had visited in our dreams.

THE DEATH OF THE DREAM

What happened to the Place Up North once my father could no longer make the trip? His grandsons, who often went there for weekends with my parents when their parents were busy getting divorced, had idealized it into their own version of the Place Up North, where everyone was nice and got along, a kind of cleansing from all the crap they had to deal with when they were young—too young to understand. They loved building campfires there, and fishing in the stream (though one of them finally noticed that there was no hook on his line, just the rubber worm my father had tied on).

The boys wanted the place—at least the dream of it, so my father turned the title over to them. Frankly, they seem to have neglected to notice all the work my father was doing while they played in the stream and woods. They have not kept the place up, by all reports. The mice have taken over. The complex and illegal water and sewage system has fallen beyond disrepair. The roof of the built-on room has separated from the trailer, causing leaks. It's so unsightly that neighbors have complained to my father in writing, and that's saying a lot, given the state of the other ramshackle dwellings lining the creek. The long-distance dream of the Place Up North has fallen on hard times, blurred by the naïve nostalgia of grandchildren. A literal ruin to begin with has now become both a literal and figurative nightmare. City kids like us knew little about the natural world, so we idealized it, like Francophiles or Anglophiles. Tip-toeing through poison ivy has its long-term consequences.

THE PERMANENT MOON OF THE STREETLIGHT

I've got my own nostalgia to deal with. The one thing that did survive on our lawn: the streetlight. The old creosote pole, worn and splintered, yet still erect, in the corner of our old front yard. No concern for its branchless trunk, no concern about falling leaves. No, just the one branch of metal arcing out of the wood with its one blossom of light hanging its moon over the street, dutifully punctuating dusk, then night, as it has for over sixty years.

This, this was our true tree, our reliable urban tree that needed no caring, that would live forever (with the occasional changing of the light bulb). A beacon of light, the mast of our docked ship of cement and brick. The streetlight was like the mysterious black monolith in *2001: A Space Odyssey* with the apes swarming madly around it. We were the apes, and the streetlight was the monolith. It attracted us as a mysterious beacon of possibility.

NO TICKETS NECESSARY

We were inventors of our own amusement. Magicians—it looked like nothing was there, but when we said the secret words and blinked, we made magic.

During the summer, when it got dark later, we'd hang out after dinner in random groups—in a jumble beneath the streetlight or circling on our bicycles—and play a game in which whoever first noticed the streetlights had come on shouted "First on the Streetlights." Deceptively and un-deceptively simple. The prize was momentary recognition of some kind of observational prowess. You could shout "Second on the Street-lights," or "Third," but you weren't first, so it didn't really matter. How gray did the sky need to get to trigger them? Often, the color of the sky matched the color of the cement, and we were sandwiched between those gray layers.

After the interruption of our streetlight shouting, we continued doing whatever we'd been doing, which was often nothing. Talking smack—we did that a lot. Swearing. Talking dirty. Or, alternately, revealing our vulnerability with confidences that were not shared beyond our misshapen circle. We acknowledged the streetlight as a mysterious power. It gave light, it had symmetry and substance in its perfect direct roundness. It connected us. Maybe we imagined warmth, since it had no warmth. Or was it personal warmth? The community of lost souls awaiting puberty, or trying to figure out what to do upon its rude arrival.

Even in winter, we spent a lot of time outdoors. Or, maybe especially in winter, given the tiny houses, the large families, the lack of privacy. We accepted our ignorance of nature and lack of curiosity to know more. What value did it have? What did it have to do with our lives? All we knew was that it was winter and we were cold. May as well hit each other with snowballs. Or wash each other's faces in snow, one of our winter humiliations.

At night, when the streetlight was on and the snow was good packing, the temperature hovering around freezing, maybe slightly above, we threw snowballs at the streetlight in a game that had no name—it started and ended spontaneously. The goal was to hit the pole with your snowball at the highest point in its arc, and, thus, leave the highest white mark on the dark pole. This involved some accuracy and a good throwing arm. And persistence. Maybe even some math to figure out the proper angle and distance so that your snowball would hit the—I almost wrote tree!—pole at maximum height.

We could do this for an amazingly long time. It seemed like right when we were ready to give up, someone would make a lucky heave and raise the bar again, inspiring the rest of us to keep trying. Apes paying tribute to the pole. The game could go on forever—no one could ever reach the top of the pole under that magical light as bright as at a night baseball game. And after all, we had an endless supply of balls.

THE SUBSTANCE OF LIGHT

Ah, the streetlight. The streetlight! I learned from my parents years later that the developers tried to persuade other neighbors to allow them to put one in front of their houses. No, the others said, it'll put out too much light. It'll attract noise and nighttime activities—well, this part is true, since us four moth-like boys were responsible for attracting a lot of moth-like activities.

The odd thing was that when things started to get unsafe— my own mother mugged in our driveway returning from work late one night—the neighbors rushed to put up floodlights in an attempt to keep nighttime badness at bay. It'll shine in our windows, and we won't be able to sleep, they'd said, but then the darkness kept them up.

Our wise parents could keep an eye on us just by looking out the window as we fluttered in that bright light. They said *yes*, and the streetlight was placed on the edge of the lawn next to our neighbor's driveway. The Seleskis, an older, quiet, childless couple who were also our party-line partners, suffered inside and out from the noisy evidence of us five kids. Ours was the third house from the corner, which also had a streetlight. If you drive down the street—or take a stroll down Google Maps—you'll see an unnatural gap between streetlights, the dark droop in the middle of the block, where, given the symmetry of everything else, you'd expect a light.

On the edge of that lawn, it still stands. Our streetlight—on our property! We took a strange reasonless pride in that, and when giving directions, we always said, we're in the house with the streetlight.

The streetlight served as a neighborhood signpost, billboard. The last time I was home before my parents moved, I examined the pole littered with old nails and thumbtacks that had held up 8½ x 11 sheets to announce candy sales, garage sales, lost pets, babysitting opportunities, etc. Those bumpy, rusty pieces of metal told the braille history of our street. I ran my hand over them and briefly wept—I'd tacked up a few of those sheets myself. The streetlight had been goal in all our childhood games. The safe space. We could touch it and instantly feel the relief of certainty. I pulled my hand off it, then wiped my eyes and turned back to my own children waiting in the car with my wife to make the long drive back to Pittsburgh.

Once, my hand touched goal on top of Cindy Wisneski's in simultaneous connection. Our warm hands lingered together. I was never the same.

THE WOODS AND *THE* FIELD

While we had multiple car washes, gas stations, fast-food joints, and churches, all natural areas were singular.

Woods

The problem with having no tree to climb is that you have no tree to climb. Nothing to give perspective on the whole thing—whatever thing that is—the Monopoly board of the street, neighborhood, the balding heads of our fathers, the roots of our mothers' dyed hair, babushkas of our grandmothers, the pulling in and pulling out of identical cars in front of identical houses, the invisible magnets beneath the streets pulling them along inevitably to the factory gate in some board game not called LIFE. It was even an expression on the street: *Oh, go climb a tree*, where there were no trees to climb. In other words, disappear. Be gone.

The closest trees to climb were isolated in a small, wooded cluster next to Schofield Elementary School. We called this area "The Woods." It had legendary status because those trees offered one of the few places within miles that was wild enough to hide in, to disappear into. As teenagers, we used it as a place to guzzle apple wine and smoke weak pot and imagine we were stoned. We could be alone with girls there, kissing against bark, the smell of damp earth rising like a soundtrack to kissing. You might see a squirrel or rabbit. Or even a rat.

The Woods, where thick, old trees could not be trusted to hold us up, keep us alive, and thus gave us an opportunity to be reckless, to wedge dirt and grime beneath our fingernails and grind it into our palms. We were drawn to the lack of trust, the twisted trunks, the sagging branches. No one taught us how to climb trees. We used monkey-bar techniques and hoped for the best. Hoped for a soft landing after the inevitable fall.

Field

We took a shortcut to and from school every day, cutting through our homemade baseball diamond in The Field at the end of Otis Street and behind Bach Street, a rocky, weedy lot left undeveloped, skipped over in the mad rush of developers into suburbia on their manifest destiny to build out as far away from Detroit as they could. It may have had something to do with zoning. I'm sure it had something to do with money.

The path became a river of mud in rainstorms, and slick, icy ruts in snowstorms, and we loved its rowdy mess and disorder. We branched off from the sidewalk down into the field at Otis when the sidewalk ended. Fights were fought on that shortcut, kisses were kissed. We fell off bikes, landing on the softer earth. We felt like we were getting over on someone somehow by not using the sidewalk. By getting our good shoes muddy and tracking it into school.

But all shortcuts eventually disappear. They built a tool and die shop and fenced off their parking lot, which cut us off, forcing us to take the longer sidewalk route, closer to traffic, confined to those narrow gray squares, humiliated by puddle and slush spray that was not of our own making.

DIAMOND IN THE ROUGH

One magical day, a telephone pole on the edge of the field offered us a gift. A repairman had climbed it with his special spiked boots, hoisting himself up on the nearly invisible steps—rods of bent metal stuck out on either side of the pole. We'd never seen a man climb higher, except on televised lumberjack segments some Saturday afternoons on *Wide World of Sports*. When we saw a green Bell Telephone van, we always stopped to watch the workers climb up and down. We had no idea what they were doing up there. Not electrocuting themselves, I guess, despite live wires and heights and the flimsy belt they leaned back into while they worked. They went higher than the roofs of our one-story houses. Minor gods in their safety gear. Sometimes they even whistled while they worked.

That day, after the Bell Telephone guy got in his chariot and drove off, we noticed a pile of bundles of thin purple wire on the ground beneath the pole. Obviously, a gift from the gods. What to do with this gift?

We played baseball for years on our personal diamond in The Field. The whole subdivision had once been one local farm, and The Field was all that was left. The farmer's house still stood, with one tiny plot the ancient farmer couple continued to plant behind their house until they died. In front of their small house stood one tiny, twisted crabapple tree. Every fall we picked up the fallen ones and fired them at each other. What damage we did was to each other. That's what we got from trees: ammunition.

When we were quite young—first or second graders?—we'd created an asymmetrical baseball diamond, with home plate resting beneath the one large remaining tree someone left as a joke or afterthought. The distances between bases were way off. We hit many doubles, but few triples. You had to pack a lunch to make it from second to third.

A few years later, we decided to make it right. We foraged our father's workbenches for tools, then measured the bases and buried cinderblocks to ground level ninety feet apart, still keeping home plate in front of that one tree. We'd stolen the blocks from some nearby building project that would become our neighborhood's first convenience store. We built up a pile of mud into an actual pitcher's mound and buried another brick there to make a concrete rubber. Our diamond was in the great American tradition of the sandlot, but our lot ended up being a tight squeeze—we had to measure everything to fit into the model railroad village of the boxed grid of the neighborhood.

The field was so full of milkweed and Queen Anne's lace that we often lost balls in the high weeds—particularly the long balls. Or, worse, we pretended to lose the balls so that home runs became ground-rule doubles. The solution? A home-run barrier consisting of pieces of random sticks and lumber scraps driven into the ground that were connected by those purple wires braided together. Over the wires was a home run. To be honest, when the weeds grew higher, the barrier morphed into a trip wire for careless and enthusiastic outfielders. Still, for a time, we had our own barrier, one we'd made ourselves, and we all agreed on what was a home run.

When we outgrew our field and could hammer balls out into the busy traffic of Ryan Road, we briefly ventured into arson in our endless quest to make our mark. We had matches and cigarette lighters, and our first cigarettes. We'd start the dry weeds on fire and stand in excited fear as we watched it grow, daring each other to wait a second longer than last time before we all madly stomped the fire out just before it spread out of control. It only took the fire department coming out once to stop that amusement. The burned part grew back, erasing that mark like all the others. Making our mark seemed like a full-time job, yet it was amazing how quickly the damage disappeared.

A couple of years later, they dug up the weeds and took down that one tree, the one we idled under while waiting our turns to bat on hot summer days, and built Bronco Lanes, filling in the final patch left after the tool and die shop had cut off the shortcut. What did we do? We shrugged, then we signed up for a bowling league like our parents did, and we learned how to play arcade games, wasting our paper route money in the tiny game room. Our one piece of natural shade was gone forever, but leveling had its compensations. Ask the man with the chainsaw.

SAD AVIARY OF MISFIT BIRDS

When climbed, those old trees in The Woods, and that one in The Field, allowed a bird's eye view of the identical roofs of our houses. Bird's eye—just an expression. I'm not sure what bird's eyes we saw with, but I'm guessing sparrow. We had sparrows, and more sparrows. Sometimes a robin with its exotic flash or orange—the state bird, though apparently most of them lived up north. And the even rarer mirage of a cardinal. And the miraculous seagulls that occasionally landed in the A&P parking lot, drifting over from Lake St. Clair, or perhaps even from Canada. Maybe they imagined the parking lot was a frozen lake. The arrival of gulls was a strange, wondrous sight, which drove us to run and shout to make them scatter and caw their foreign language. We knew they were foreigners. It was our concrete beach.

One year for my birthday, my mother gave me two dime-store parakeets, thinking I needed something to befriend, given that my two pairs of siblings were close in age, clumped together in the distance on both sides of me. The first bird died after two days. My mother got a small mirror to keep the other one company, but it too died by the end of that first week, and the cage quickly disappeared. It seemed like both inside and out, we were cluelessly killing everything natural.

In Cub Scouts, one of our den mothers had us weave baskets as an activity. I chose to make a bird's nest, which was tricky, given the suggested symmetry of the circular nest and the square hole for birds to enter. The whole thing ended up predictably misshapen, nevertheless I gifted it to my mother. It never saw the light of day. She attached a couple of tiny fake nameless birds to it with wire and inserted it into one of the nooks in the living room as part of her spring-themed display—an array of birds on various shelves—ceramic, glass, Styrofoam—cardinal, blue jay, robin (I've never seen a fake sparrow). The birds were safe in those wooden squares. They'd be up until fall when the pumpkin display took over. My mother dusted the birds before putting them up each spring. Dusting birds. It was something we were capable of doing—just not keeping them alive.

SAFETY FIRST

Our toy arrows were useless on those streets, with their rubber-suction tips that stuck to literally nothing. With our tiny dime-store plastic bows, we were mean little cupids, frustrated by our inability to put holes in anything, to make a mark or dent into the concrete and brick surrounding us like walls of a fort that were keeping us in or keeping us out. Only our father's masonry drill bit could penetrate.

Once, we tried peashooters, then, after the next rain, the idle sprouts erupted on lawns, greener than the grass, evidence of our many misses. Slingshots were more our style—the possibility of actual wounds. Yo-yos were mocked because of their showy cleverness and boring lack of consequence. Balsawood planes? Ridiculous. Seconds after you slid the wings into the slot on the fuselage and tossed it into the air, no matter how you adjusted the metal clip on the plane's nose, it dove into the cement street of its own demise. Kites offered their brief delirium of sky. No trees to bring them down, but plenty of electrical wires. Frisbees landed on roofs and never came down.

SELF-DESTRUCT: Echo, echo, echo

What did it mean to us to not have reliable trees? As much as we loved the streetlight—its muted buzz illuminating our young script of swear words and bullshit, bravado and weakness, secrets and lies nourished by the light—our imaginations took a hit under its honest scrutiny, and our words echoed hollow, nearly visible, off cement. No current of leaves to mute our hushed whispers. No volume control for illumination or wonder. Wonder took a backseat, looking for a place to put down roots. To find a consistent thread of metaphor.

I think the lack of trees egged on our mean, destructive tendencies. Our bikes, then our cars, plowed into street signs and parked vehicles. We relied too heavily on curbs to stop us with their inconsequential jolts. We bounced over curbs with abandon. Once we were able to drive, we did "lawn jobs" in front of our enemies' houses. With no trees to stop us, we recklessly drove over curbs to rip up grass, gouging muddy tire tracks, as we swerved back into the street and sped away. The nicer the lawn, the greater the satisfaction.

In addition to lawn jobs, we did "bleach jobs," a more public and blatant display of aggression that involved pouring bleach on your tires, and/or on the street, then doing burnouts to lay rubber. The bleach made the tires shed more and leave larger skid marks, sprouting huge clouds of black smoke. The squealing tires, revving engines, the smoke, the stinging smell of burning rubber—all made us feel like drag racers, despite driving rusty transportation specials.

Just one living tree might have been good enough for us. A tree can orient lives around it to the cycle of its seasons. My father tried a couple of trees in the backyard too. Once, in a fit of naïve madness, he bought a tree with branches of four different kinds of apples grafted onto it. He didn't understand or realize that he had to use pesticides in order for the apples to ripen without getting worms or bugs, to grow and be edible. The tree gave us a few wormy ones, which, of course, we threw at each other, then the whole tree rotted, a stunted, deformed Frankenstein monster, and met the same fate as the trees out front.

MIRACLE-GRO

Hardly anyone in the neighborhood ever planted anything you could eat, though the adventurous sometimes tried tomatoes in the summer to put on those burgers we'd be grilling—even we recognized the tastelessness of store-bought tomatoes. My father, the master green-thumber, sometimes threw a few scraggly plants in the yard next to the fence bordering the Seleskis' house, now occupied by an immigrant couple from Russia. The husband, whose limited knowledge of English had not kept him from getting a job on the line at Chrysler's (my friends and I also counted on getting those jobs with their simple qualifications), planted tomatoes on his side of the cyclone fence. Some summer Saturdays, he and my father had crude limited conversations about whose tomato plants were better and who would get the first ripe tomato. Then, in one of the highlights of my father's life, he got an idea: he tied a ripe store-bought tomato to one of his plants with thread. He kept an eye out the window for the old Russian to come out into his yard, and soon enough it happened: the man stood there, hands on hips, shaking his head at the tomato as if it had been a bad boy—not a Big Boy or Better Boy. I'd never seen my father laugh so hard.

REVISIONIST HISTORY

In the backyard of my grandfather's house on the East Side of Detroit, one old, gnarled tree grew crooked on a gradually sloped angle beside the fence next to the alley—gradual enough for small boys—and thus it earned its name as The Climbing Tree, the one tree we could safely get up into. We straddled the trunk and scooched up, imagining we were riding a horse.

The same tree my father had climbed as a boy, along with his brother who died in high school before outgrowing it.

My father and I sometimes drive around his old neighborhood, in the bruised heart of Detroit. The last time we made the trip, the gradual destruction of the block, abandoned house by abandoned house, had been completed, with every house leveled. This counted as a success for the city, which continues to have a backlog of empty houses to knock down. Someone had planted trees in the weeds and rubble as part of a reforestation project to shrink the city's footprint, get more territory off the grid, return it to the wilds. Reduce services. Save money. But as we drove past, we could see those new trees already dying, dead leaves clinging to their crooked, spindly branches. We idled briefly on the corner, trying to estimate how far down their house had been. No landmarks left to help us find our bearings. If this were a story in search of a happy ending, we would have found the climbing tree and been inspired by its survival, but the dirt and gravel alley it bordered had also disappeared long ago. We were heartened a bit just by the failed attempt to plant trees. My father empathized—after all, he hadn't had success himself, except for the giant pine.

THE FAMOUS TREES OF DALLAS STREET

Our shortcut to school emptied out onto Dallas, an older street on the border of our subdivision which had been part of Warren Township, a sleepy farmland, long before it became the third largest city in the state. Near the main crossroads of Ryan and Nine Mile Roads, Dallas had substantial trees on its larger lots—larger lots, though even smaller houses than ours, cottages really. The narrow street had no parking or sidewalks, just drainage ditches on either side of the blacktop. One of the largest trees on Dallas, The Crunchy Tree, dropped thick brown leaves that we rode our bikes over in the fall. We considered it worth the ride to make those crunches and crackles, pulverizing

those leaves against the street. Maybe it was our gateway drug
to lawn jobs and bleach jobs. An old woman lived alone in
the house behind the tree. Her house was dark on Halloween.
We called her a witch. Our ignorance operated on so many
levels—we found it around every corner.

The other famous Dallas tree—one I could identify!—was
the giant weeping willow at the end of the shortcut. We pushed
through the curtains of that tree, and suddenly we were on the
busy stage on Ryan Road, clogged with traffic at shift changes
that corresponded with our school day. We called it The Tarzan
Tree, fantasizing about grabbing a handful of vines and swinging from tree to tree. Except there was no next tree to swing
to. *Tree*, singular— though even pushing ourselves through
the thin hanging vines was dream-like, surrounding us briefly
in green curtains. The vines hung low, dusting the sidewalk in
the breeze. I once made a couple of feeble attempts at flying,
but when I grabbed a handful of branches, they just sagged to
the sidewalk, not sustaining even my meager weight. After all,
the tree was busy weeping.

DOGWOOD DAYS AND DOG DAYS

I know it might seem preposterous, but I sometimes wonder
if our lives would have been softened somehow by a few more
trees on Rome Street. If, in their shade, our cruelty to each
other would not have heated up and burned into random
destructive fury. We were not taught to nurture, and we did
not need to be taught to destroy. Many of us seemed satisfied
with random bullying and vandalism, pointless theft, drunken
driving, weapons, drugs.

Our high school had no courses in tree identification or
anything that explored the natural world, so after leaf collect-
ing in grade school, our education in nature was over. Instead,
we could take a class called Drugs, Delinquency, and Disorder, which attempted to meet us where we were at. That, and

Outdoor Chef, which advocated for the liberal use of charcoal lighter fluid, and which proved to be very popular, both with the vo-tech crowd and the nerd-crowd. Grilling burgers and hot dogs on cement patios—we all knew it would be part of our futures.

I moved away from Rome over forty years ago, and in those years, I have had some limited success with not only identifying but growing trees. Not hugging them, but appreciating them as I begin the passage through my own final seasons. At 68, I have started counting sideways, not just up, looking to leave some greenery behind, some fruit to pick. Or at least not kill the trees I inherited. My favorite is a dogwood in the front yard of our first house in hilly Pittsburgh, the tree surrounded by green ivy running down the quick slope to the retaining wall next to the sidewalk. The previous owner had been in the Mafia, according to his surviving relatives, and had used his downtown flower shop as a front, but his wife had taken her nourishment from the yard and trees. The first year after we moved in, she sent us a Christmas card with an old photo tucked inside of the dogwood in bloom. My tree, she called it, though she never came back to visit.

Five matching windows across the front of the living room looked out onto the dogwood as it did its seasonal thing: white flowers tinged with green in spring; variegated leaves, light green on darker green, through the summer; red leaves of autumn shot into brilliance with sun on the rare clear Pittsburgh day; surprise winter ice storms, the snow wet enough to stick to branches, then freeze over into crystal. My brother-in-law Andy, a gardener for a nearby university, taught me how to trim the dead branches and thin it out every year, and I like to think I helped keep it alive.

I used to say when the tree died, we'd sell the house. Thirty-five years we lived there, and the tree continued to have nothing but good things to say. The other color the tree took on was the man-made drippings of white outdoor semi-gloss I used to paint the gutters and the soffit and facia out front. The tree survived getting mangled by my clumsy ladder placement as I squeezed between branches. It survived neighbors who had admired our tree. No one had a tree as old and beautiful on the block. It outlived the childhoods of our children, my job, the drug dealers across the street, the hoarder in the house next door. And it may outlive me, downsized like my father into a small condo a few miles from that old house. It pains me as I write this in spring to know that the dogwood is blooming now, and that I will not go back to visit.

To further cement my ignorance on the tree front—cement being my favorite comparison—we also inherited a tree in the small backyard when we bought that house, a tree that put out small red fruit we first thought were cherries. Andy, with his associate's degree in forestry from Penn State, and his gentle humor and tolerance for my ignorance, informed us it was an ornamental crabapple. He still called it The Cherry Tree for years, even after it died—yes, I did kill that one—even after we moved away. He recommended a serviceberry tree to replace it and helped me plant it. We ate those berries when we were able to beat the birds to them. Good on cereal, and worth the effort to pick.

I wonder, am I bragging about my ignorance, as we did back on the street, mocking kids for carrying books home from school to do homework? Why were we drawn to the random destruction of all things natural, even while benefiting from the escape they offered? Was it the intoxicating lure of power? The power of the primitive? The power to prove we were as hard as those streets we walked on, as the metal cars we drove? We carried knives, flicking their blades at the air or each other's feet. Nothing to whittle. No sharpened sticks, just the flash of blades. Our cars, urban beasts, grunted on the lone prairies without hiding places. The hard exposure of cement. No give. If trees had lights...Trees do have lights. But we need the unreliable sun to turn on those lights.

All these years later, I still wrestle with that prideful ignorance. Despite the occasional spindly tree, the two surreal green
patches of Mr. B. and Crazy Eddie, the ragged sprays of dandelions and clover, the seasonal sprouts from pea shooters, the
unchanging streetlights and fire hydrants were our redwoods
and mushrooms. Markers. Trail markers to keep from getting
lost on those identical streets where no one trusted anyone they
didn't already know. Due to the lack of trees, dogs fought over
the sparse but permanent fire hydrants as a place to piss, to
temporarily mark their territory, just like me and my brothers
and our friends marked ours.

We had no rake among our yard tools—raking would have
made the list of chores if we had leaves to rake. If we'd had
a tree, would we have carved our initials in it? Or would we
have cut it down for kicks? We were comfortable in our creosote coats, protected from the life cycle on our static streets.
Strangely, despite the exception of the legendary dogwood, this
ignorance of trees has followed me through life. Drop me in a
car anywhere in the Detroit metropolitan area, and I'm going
to easily find my way home. Put me in a city park the size of
a postage stamp, and I'll find a way to get lost.

SEED OF DESTRUCTION

To be honest, I think some of my frustration came from an
inability to get lost. Late and alone one drunken night, I stole
a bowling ball from Bronco Lanes and rolled it down Otis and
into traffic on Ryan. What possessed me to do such a reckless,
dangerous thing? I still can hear the sound of it clonking over
the rough cement. I wish I could imagine that ball as a hard
husk waiting to be cracked open to give rise to a new tree—like
an acorn or a chestnut or a monkey ball—but that nut was
impossible to crack, protecting its core of nothing, designed
only to knock things down. A bowling ball, can you imagine
it? Otis, a wide lane without gutters. The ball clutched in my

hands, I stepped forward and released it. I can see it rolling into the busy street and disappearing in the distance—the hard knot of my heart thrown recklessly into the night.

LIGHT POLLUTION

While on the subject of drunken nights, I often arrived home seasick, clutching that mast of the streetlight to keep my balance. All I could do was hold on. Some mornings, my brothers and I staggered home to be first *off* the streetlights as they blinked into the gray morning sleep we were headed towards.

I know it's perverse to celebrate a tree cut down and stripped by man, instead of honoring natural growth. Why do I still miss that streetlight? From the distance of time, it looks like the same one on Google Maps. Sure, the streetlight blocked out stars, competed with the moon, abstracted the sky, lowering the ceiling close enough to our raised heads so we could hear the buzzing bulb in its glow and smell the creosote honey. It gave us sweetness in lieu of moony dreams or taught us to limit those dreams. As the street silenced into sleep, the buzzing remained, echoing comfort into our sleep. Under that light, we were safe. We were lucky. We counted the blessings of that sober light, in lieu of our old, memorized prayers. We wore our haloes at a tilt.

Oh, the halo of Saint Streetlight, beneficent in its protective glow. It was our urban campfire gathering circle, to tell stories, to give each other shit, to sniff and bark at each other in that lack of warmth. To find a partner to lead into the darkness where real warmth could be stolen. That creosoted pole looked down on us with warmth and generosity, or at least a complete lack of judgment.

REAL ARTIFICIAL

Knowing the names of things doesn't necessarily change anything, but knowing someone's name is one way we create recognition and familiarity. I wish I had been able to slow down enough to become familiar, if not intimate, with trees—in front of our houses, in our fields, in our woods, and in the great Up North.

For many years, my wife, my children, and I cut down our Christmas tree, driving into the country outside Pittsburgh and making a day of it. The smell of pine in my own house, lit by the glass bulbs of my childhood that I'd inherited, reminded me of family Christmases when I was young. When our children grew up and moved away, a real tree was no longer a priority. We got an artificial tree on sale one year after the holidays, and it looks real enough, the lights permanently attached—the whole erecting process taking only minutes. No need for those *water the tree* notes I used to write myself, no need to constantly try to collect the dropping needles. That's what kind of tree we have, an Artificial.

Back when we got a real tree, every year my daughter used to add a small handful of fallen needles to a glass box kept in the top drawer of our buffet. Every so often, I'd go in the drawer for something else and find myself taking off the lid to take a whiff.

When we were packing to move into our small condo—no grass to mow, no trees—I hesitated slightly before dumping the box of needles in the trash, knowing I'd miss the memories evoked by the smell. Now, we buy candles that smell like pine trees and light them at Christmas time—artificial has no odor.

While you might say, *Oh, go climb a tree,* I do regret my ignorance of the natural world, the layers of cement and blacktop and brick covering the streets, rising on top of each other to lower curbs, making it less and less possible to return to earth, the original script, feet in the dirt, spreading roots, or moving, kicking up dirt. Feet on the ground.

It's only a matter of time before somebody cuts down that giant pine on Rome. If it falls, it'll crush the roof of the old house or knock down the power lines. It's a miracle it hasn't already gotten tangled in the wires connecting the telephone pole to the streetlight. I take what the world gives me, use it up, destroy it. I embrace the wooden poles with all their slivers. I take the light from streetlights to see in the dark.

For years, I had to go inside when the streetlight came on. What will happen when it goes off and never comes on again? Who will be left to call Last on the Streetlights?

Oh, who am I kidding? Lying in bed late at night, trying to fall asleep, I still recite the names of cars.

THE ABRIDGED
BOOK OF WATER

In Michigan, you are never more than six miles from a body of water.

Warren is an inner-ring suburb of Detroit. According to the United States Census Bureau, the city has a total area of 34.46 square miles (89.25 km), of which 34.38 square miles (89.04 km) is land and 0.08 square miles (0.21 km) is water.

What water was within *our* six-mile radius? I imagine a dowser with his magic stick wandering our concrete wasteland on the edge of Detroit for that .08. Perhaps that is the accumulated total of the water in all the above-ground swimming pools in Warren, Michigan. A body of water. Oh, to be, to have, a body of water! As kids, our dreams were limited to what we could walk or ride our bikes to, in search of that elusive water. In our neighborhood beside Eight Mile Road, the border with Detroit, we were thirteen miles from the Detroit River, the most likely candidate. We lacked dowsing sticks, or sticks of any kind, and the occasional scrap of a two-by-four didn't have the supple subtlety to bend with hope and faith.

You might think that growing up in the "Water-Winter Wonderland" state, the "Great Lakes" state, the "Great Lakes, Great Times" state," the "Say Yes to Michigan" state, the "Pure

Michigan," state (the most recent and inscrutable slogan), with the state motto of "If You Seek a Pleasant Peninsula, Look About You," that we would not crave swimming pools, given the wealth of lakes lapping the edges of our Mitten. The "Mitten State" (who ever wore mittens to go swimming?). These slogans might suggest that proximity equals access. And thus, we come to the great (not Great) myth of the "Place Up North", in which nearly every autoworker in the Detroit area dreams of having enough money to buy a Place Up North on a river or lake to get away for weekends and vacations and, someday, retirement. To get close to a body of water that you could then claim access to, whether that involved swimming, boating, fishing, or drowning.

I'VE LIVED MY ENTIRE LIFE without a swimming pool. In retrospect, thank God. In our family that included five children, a deaf grandmother, a harried mother, and an absent father working massive amounts of overtime at the nearby Ford factory, having a pool would have been a recipe for disaster that even an aquatic Betty Crocker could not safely fix: who could invite friends over to swim? When? Was the concept of sharing viable when even four people could crowd the typical aboveground pool?

I'm sure we all, at one time or another, broached the topic with our parents: "Can we get a swimming pool?" On those sweltering summer days when we sat on our bikes on some random spot on the street waiting for the ice cream truck to show up, having a pool was often a topic of discussion and fantasy. We amused ourselves by creating our own flat pyramid scheme. We sold glasses of Kool-Aid for a nickel a glass to adults on the street who took pity on us, then we turned around and used the money to buy a popsicle from the ice cream man for a dime.

Discussions with my father about getting a pool were short and not sweet. He'd interrupt any whiny discourse by going on about the amount of work that went into having a pool. And then, looking at me, he'd point out that I couldn't even clean up the dog crap in the yard on a regular basis, so how was I going to be capable of keeping a pool clean. "But, but," I'd stutter. "But nothing," he'd say, detailing the expense, upkeep, and safety a pool required. The chemicals, the filter. The bug skimmer, the ladder. And who was going to be the lifeguard? By all reports, no one liked taking care of a pool. Nobody had a pool boy in our neighborhood. We were all pool boys.

Pool filters hummed. None of us hummed like that. Our humming was a mechanical process, like the box fans that blew hot air around our tiny houses. The pool-filter hum, on the other hand, was like the sound of a rare bird. I can hear it still in dreams of childhood. No one had air conditioning, with its very loud hum. We didn't speak air-conditioning. We had to go to the movie theater for our taste of it, that foreign film without subtitles.

In our fantasies, we imagined the pool instantly full, clean, to cool us off on the hottest days. In reality, it took days to fill a pool, a green garden hose hanging limply over the edge. And once it was full, the water was ice-cold for weeks. Anticipation, followed by more anticipation. And rain just made it colder. In between hot, muggy days, we had cool, rainy days. After all, this was Detroit, not Miami.

IN OUR NEIGHBORHOOD, only three houses had backyard pools. Their stories were all different, and all the same, for having a pool was like a bribe or a barrier (or both) in terms of fitting into our tight-knit—and simply tight (or uptight!)—community, houses squeezed in next to each other like postage stamps on a small thick envelope.

Imagine an aerial view of a swimming pool on a postage stamp, one small round blue circle behind the orange squares of identical brick houses. Your eyes would be drawn to that blue dot like it was a magic coin. We had three blue dots in our neighborhood, the pools all circular, above-ground, four-feet deep, standard size: 52 inches high, 24 feet in diameter. Three, a magic number—our third eye allows us imagination, right? Three pools, creating their bold, contained chaos of roundness in our square world. Three blue eyeballs encased in plastic and vinyl and aluminum. No one in our working-class neighborhood could afford a built-in pool. If somebody constructed an in-ground pool like those sleek rectangles we sometimes saw outside next to motels on long drives or on *The Beverly Hillbillies* TV show, our heads would have exploded. "A cee-ment pond!" we'd have shouted, with the exuberance of Jethro Bodine.

INTRODUCING SWIMMING POOLS to the neighborhood created the shock of simply seeing each other's uncovered skin. The usual, even on the hottest days, was long pants—jeans—and t-shirts. We had trucker tans that stopped where our short sleeves started. Nobody wore shorts. Our parents would not buy us shorts—they added a whole new expense, times however many kids you had. At some point in our early teens, we were allowed to cut off jeans that had the knees blown out anyway and wear those as shorts. Why were pre-made shorts considered pretentious? Perhaps because our factory-worker fathers never wore shorts. Richie Rich, of comic book fame, he wore shorts.

ON OCCASION, I was allowed the privilege of handling the skimmer to remove dead bugs from someone's pool, which was its own calming Zen-like experience (saving bug lives while making the pool [world] a better place for swimmers [me and you]), but I was an outsider to the land of pools, which meant I paid keen attention to the insiders. And maybe it meant I was a chump for doing my friends' work. Lying in bed at night, I would imagine the brief, calm blue mirage of clean water. Ah, I'd think, falling into blue dreams, if only!

POOL 1: THE ROMANOS

MRS. ROMANO WAS the Great Tanned Shark of the street. She commanded that pool in her gold metal-flake bikini. She has to come first here because she always came first. Her husband, Big Tony, the father, was a short, stout guy who looked like somebody had chiseled him out of granite or poured him into a cement mold. He did not work at the plant. He came and went until he finally went forever, leaving the house to Lucia and the boys. Was the swimming pool a desperate gesture of apology, a way of paying tribute, or part of some bargain she'd made with Mr. Romano that went wrong?

MRS. ROMANO DIDN'T FIT in our neighborhood of factory workers—even when she became one of those workers herself, the only woman on the block who worked the line at Ford's. She named her kids Michael and Angelo—Mich(a)el-Angelo, though no one ever mentioned that artistic connection. Surely, some of our parents knew about Michelangelo, even if none of us kids did. If we did, it might have created a tool for mockery, the primary tool we used to screw each other up, to poke holes, to strip those screws—our tool was a multi-purpose one. Like a Swiss Army knife, though no one had one of those either. The comb-switchblade combo was coveted. Not that anyone ever used their blade, but flicking it out now and then helped pass the time while waiting for someone to invite us over to swim in their pool.

What we did know, and could see with our own enlarged, glazed-over eyeballs, was Mrs. Romano's gold metal-flake bikini. As far as I knew, none of our mothers ever even had a bikini, much less looked good in one, or wore one in public. Trying to imagine it made me cringe.

The Romanos never built a garage, and if I go on Google Earth, I can see that whoever lives there now hasn't built one either. Or, if I just go on regular earth, doing an old-neighborhood drive-by with my father hunched in the seat beside me, pleased to have finally moved out of there, but also pleased to lift the old names out of the hat in his lap and recite them like a show-off first grader. He's in his nineties, bent on assuring us his memory is still functioning.

"Lucia Romano," he says, unprompted. "When she retired from Ford's and moved to Florida, she gave me a good-bye kiss on the lips. On the lips," he repeats, to emphasize its significance in our buttoned-up neighborhood. He groans—or maybe moans, his old-man noises blurring. He rearranges himself in the uncomfortable passenger seat of my little blue Focus. He has to take off his baseball cap just to get in.

"I got her the job at the plant," he says.

"I know," I say.

THE ROMANOS' POOL may have been the first on the block. A mirage right in front of us, appearing in a yard where a garage should be. No garage, but they had a pool—what was that all about? Ask Mrs. Romano. With no garage, they had room for a pool. The houses were in such close proximity and the lots so small that once you put up a garage, pool options were limited.

My mother once got a little blow-up kiddie pool maybe a foot deep and put it on the driveway apron in front of our garage for my younger siblings, and for my mother to dip her toes in while watching them, commanding that wet little boat with her beer and a cigarette. Well, the boat was permanently docked, and quickly struck a leak or split a seam—inevitable, given the rough concrete it sat on.

Concrete was our dominant surface. Street and sidewalks, playgrounds. We played all the traditional games in the street. Late one night, we clandestinely painted yard lines on the street and "United States Street Football" on the fifty-yard line. Each cement slab, separated by tar spacers, represented ten yards. With such limited facilities, you might imagine the soft cool trap door a swimming pool offered.

OUR THREE POOL OWNERS were all outliers in the neighborhood, even before they got pools. The Romanos were 100% Italian on a street dominated by Polish families. Mrs. Romano became the only divorced woman on the block. She wasn't in the card club of neighborhood housewives, so they could gossip freely about her. I remember a dozen mothers at three card tables squeezed into our tiny living room, piling up cigarette butts in ashtrays we'd made as a craft in Cub Scouts, swilling beer straight from the bottles, growing louder and shriller as the night went on. In bed, I kept my ear to the wall trying to listen in. Mrs. Romano's previous modeling career got translated as "Oh, a 'model,' what kind of model was that?"

Putting in a swimming pool and inviting the neighbors over could have resulted in a lot of forgiveness, but Lucia Romano never seemed like one interested in forgiveness—for what?—and so, when the pool went in, some neighbors seemed to resent and distrust her even more. Shunned by someone they'd already shunned, they had no weapons at their disposal except the handguns hidden in their underwear drawers.

WHEN MRS. ROMANO EMERGED, unveiling the bikini heard round the world, we were stunned, staggered in our holey, stinky tennis shoes. She was tall, thin, with striking features. We could all see the model in her—whatever she'd modeled, and for who.

I'm not sure if I ever actually saw Mrs. Romano in the water, though I do remember her covered in baby oil lying on a towel in the overgrown grass next to the pool. Her olive skin shimmered like a mirage—though it was real, it was not attainable. I had to shield my eyes.

If it seems like I was a little in love with her, it's because I was. Maybe we all were, the tribe of young man-boys who hung out with her sons. We were like ants around a melting popsicle, dogs panting in the heat. Politely and quietly losing our young minds. We were a gang of lost boys, and she a hard-edged Tinkerbell who smoked and swore like an uncensored Captain

Hook. She had all her limbs. She created some confusion about our desire to cool off.

I would have been a volunteer pool boy for Mrs. Romano.

MICHAEL AND ANGELO often wandered down the street to my house to sit on the porch and be pleasantly bored while I went on about how hot it was. All I could think about was jumping in their pool. I didn't get to swim very often in the Romanos' pool, despite my various fantasies.

The pool seemed to appear overnight. Just like the pool table in their basement, which appeared to have had a previous life in some bar—we had to push in a coin slot to get the balls to appear.

THE ROMANOS HAD A SIGN on the ladder next to the tub where you washed your feet before getting in to get the dirt and grass off of them: *We don't swim in your toilet, please don't pee in our pool.* It was the first and only poem I remember from childhood—it had tension, juxtaposition, tone. It had a P word. And, I didn't quite understand it. Who would want to swim in a toilet? Go ahead and swim in my toilet, I'd say, see if I care. I think I asked her about it once and she just told me to do what the sign said and "don't pee in the damn pool."

Given my height and hers, it was hard not to stare at what was in front of me, trying to wish away my boner. "Daniels," she called me. She was the only mother to call us by our last names, and the only mother who swore in front of us. She could turn cussing into opera. I remember the high look she gave above lowered sunglasses when she was annoyed. She always gave her gum a workout. She was either smoking or chewing gum. She had no stillness in her.

One year, the Romano pool disappeared. I can't carbon-date its disappearance, but I think by then Lucia was living alone and working long hours at the plant like our fathers, with no time for laying poolside much less maintaining it. In later years, when I was home for a visit, I would sometimes see her walking around the block. Gaunt and hardened, noticeably limping, yet Mrs. Romano always had a smile and laugh for me. "Hey Daniels!" she'd say. "How you doing?" Though I never got a kiss on the lips like my dad did.

FREE SWIM

YOU MIGHT BE WONDERING if Warren had a municipal pool. The answer is no. What we had was Free Swim. Fitzgerald, our high school, had Free Swim twice a day on weekdays during the summer—a morning and afternoon session—in their indoor pool so drenched in chlorine that it turned your eyeballs bright red as soon as you walked onto the tiled deck. To get into Free Swim, we had to line up against the gym's brick wall in the blacktop-melting heat of the school parking lot. Surly, pimply lifeguards would distribute tiny orange tickets from large rolls until they hit their magic maximum number. The kids still in line were shit-out-of-luck and had to go home and jump through sprinklers with their toddler siblings.

By the time the pools started going up, most of us had outgrown those sprinklers, though at heart, we were sprinkler kids—the waving kind, not the constant spinning kind. We ran from the waving water, or jumped through it, or lay down in prickly grass and let it float over us like the sweetest rain—sweet because we could control it. We loved the swaying back and forth across tiny yards, the anticipation of seeing the wand bend toward us, the relief it brought, washing over us, and knowing it would come back the other way. The sprinkler required no invitation. Everybody had a sprinkler. Some people even watered their driveways with them. They made tiny rainbows.

WARREN, DESPITE BEING the third largest city in the state, had sprung up quickly around the auto plants in the 1950s with no thought to amenities. Warren also had no downtown—just a series of random strip malls lining the mile roads from Eight Mile to Fourteen Mile Roads (they didn't even have time to give names to their main thoroughfares), with a few after-thought postage-stamp parks on lots overlooked in the surge of development.

We got screwed on the swimming pool front. The only time the mayor showed up in our neighborhood was to assure our parents that he would not let the evil pinball people turn the abandoned gas station in the weedy field across the street from Bronco Lanes into a pinball palace. Build a goddamn cement pond, I wanted to tell him—with lifeguards and stuff!—but kids weren't allowed in the meeting. I heard that a policeman controlled the microphone and automatically cut you off after thirty seconds, and that anyone shorter than Captain Bob-Lo, the little person mascot from the amusement park on Bob-Lo Island, was not allowed to take that wild thirty-second ride. Hysteria flooded the neighborhood, so I may have some facts wrong—take them with a truckload of salt from the famous vast salt mines under the City of Detroit that spawned the working-class mantra of "Back to the salt mines" whenever it was time to return to work.

Free Swim was not free. Humiliation was the fee. The chlo-rine from Free Swim was so strong, we walked around the rest of the day with red zombie eyes. We carried our suits rolled up in our dads' old army towels—short, green, rough. We had to shower in the downstairs locker room before climbing the steps to the pool door. When we emerged into Oz, the lifeguard wizard rubbed our wrists, and if dirt came off, we had to shower up again. They clearly loved rubbing hard to make us squirm, like a mini-version of the prank called a wrist burn. Going back down the steps meant going back to a hell you thought you'd escaped—the wet, steamy, pissy locker rooms. The lifeguards were mad with power, and I understand that now—it's not like the rest of us weren't on a daily search to lord something over someone. They were almost as bad as the punk ushers at the

Ryan Theater swinging giant flashlights like billy clubs, kicking us out of the theater based on whim and boredom. I never got to see the end of *Ben-Hur*. Who won the chariot race?

POOL 2: THE ELUSIVE ELIASES

WE HAD JUST ONE Greek family on the street, the Eliases, who lived next door. They were tight with the Greek community in Detroit, headquartered in far-off Greektown, but not tight with the neighbors. We didn't even know where they went to church. They got dressed up on Sunday mornings, but when they pulled out of the driveway, they drove away from St. Mark's, the Catholic church nearly everyone else attended, and into the city. They seemed religious—polite, quiet, and mostly solemn and serious, which passed for religious on our street. Even when discussing the weather, which constituted the parents' brief exchanges with our parents. They kept to themselves, and were rarely seen outdoors—no porch sitting, no lingering. Occasionally, we'd spot Mr. E. at the hose spigot on the side of the house abutting our driveway. Their hose, was always coiled perfectly when not in use, while ours resembled a large snake sprawled across the grass. We rarely heard a peep from inside their house, despite being just a body-length away from ours. I sometimes referred to it as the Greek Monastery.

They had three daughters, who also kept (or were kept) to themselves. We didn't even know what Mr. E. did for work, but he wore a tie and white shirt when he left in the morning, was always impeccably groomed, and wafted clouds of cologne if you ever got near him. All that made him a suspect character on our street full of factory workers. A short, stocky man, Mr. Elias's voice was a high-pitched crackling howl. An oddly ethereal werewolf-like voice, like it had emerged from some robotic translating machine or language tape at school. We only had French and Spanish classes at Fitzgerald, and those were sparsely populated, and, like typing classes, filled with mostly girls. When members of their family visited, we heard snippets of Greek. Also suspicious. We never heard Mr. E. yell. What was wrong over there? It's all Greek to me!

With us four Daniels boys living next door, you'd think some cross-pollination or even harmless flirting would take place—even our father, who missed a lot of our childhoods while working in the factory, noticed the lack of cultural exchange, perhaps taking some offense on our behalf. We were one of the few Irish families in our mostly Polish neighborhood, so we had potential to share a little outsider vibe. The girls were all beautiful, but they resided on the other side of the Garden of Eden behind thick, high hedges cultivated by Mr. E. next to the cyclone fence between our yards, which gave their yard its own mystique even before the pool went up. If those girls were in it, we couldn't get a good look at them. Would bikinis be allowed? Those hedges grew through the fence and onto our side. My father took his clippers to them each summer, griping the whole time. The cyclone fences were sacred boundaries in our neighborhood, though they offered no privacy.

Why did the Eliases get a pool? These girls had successfully—I assume they'd asked for it—gotten one, and yet, it stood mostly empty. Sitting sweaty on our bikes under the meager shade of one of the few trees on the street on hot August days, we were confounded. We scratched our heads underneath our Eagles baseball hats and perhaps surreptitiously scratched our balls. We itched down there, that's for sure. Every boy on the block was on our little league team, the Eagles. We were supposed to get ice cream at the Dairy Queen when we won (though our record was 1-23 our first season, so the Dairy Queen became a kind of swimming pool for us). We knew those girls kept to themselves, and we didn't expect to get invited over, but we at least expected to hear them splashing in order to be appropriately jealous.

The Eliases's pool also seemed to appear overnight. We spied the mirage of it through those hedges one summer day from our slightly elevated kitchen casement windows above the sink, the pool squeezed between their garage and the hedges. It was often covered by a dirty plastic blue sheath that kept the water clean beneath it. A strange, giant ball sat submerged beneath the cover, making the pool look pregnant. It resembled the blue ball lawn ornament in the yard of the childless couple on Bach Street, an object of mystery and wonder whenever we caught a glimpse of it during a fence-climbing expedition to retrieve an errant ball.

AN INFAMOUS EVENT in our family history occurred when my little sister innocently cut some roses that hung through our side of the fence because she thought they were pretty. And she was right, the roses were—just like those girls—pretty, and untouchable. Getting caught by my mother with those flowers produced many tears as my mother yanked my sister over to apologize to Mrs. Elias. Humiliation all around. I still can't explain why my mother made her do it—maybe it had something to do with Mrs. E., and what seemed to be an unspoken rivalry. Mrs. E., also not a member of the card club, though since she was a ghost over there, I never heard her name come up on card club nights. The one time I heard any noise from inside that house, it was the sound of my sister wailing, traumatized, their girls mute in her hysterical presence.

Why did their pool never get used? Someone said they'd been reported for an issue with an electric wire that hung directly above it. Someone was always saying something or not saying something, which also said something about someone. Since no one knew them well, it was easy to make up theories without danger of being contradicted.

What is true is that none of us ever got invited to swim in their pool. Or to enter their house (except for The Apology). Or sit on their porch. Unfamiliarity bred suspicion—did they think they were better than us? Perhaps they were. They minded their own business. We had no business not minding our own business, but we couldn't help ourselves. We resented displays that suggested economic disparity, and we resented the stand-offishness of not sharing and acknowledging our communal lot in life. Factory workers of the world unite! Ignorance (of your neighbors) is not bliss.

THE STRANGEST THING to us was that the girls did not ride bicycles. The rest of the children—approximately eighty of us in the twenty houses on the block—practically lived on our bikes all summer, patrolling the communal cement space of the street. Everything happened there, visible, heard, our voicing magnified, echoing. We had a lot of time on our hands those summers before we could work or even get a paper route. None of us ever went to any summer camp, except for the week the Boy Scouts spent at Camp D-Bar-A. So, the street it was. What did those beautiful girls do in that closed-up house all summer, ignoring the pool in the Garden of Elias behind those hedges? Did they have an underground tunnel that allowed them to escape us? A bedroom window sat on the side of their house beside our driveway, and while I'm sure they heard a lot of our mischief, we heard none of theirs.

THE GIRLS WERE NICE—polite in school—but their vision always seemed directed somewhere above us to other possibilities in the larger world. Our world was tight, shrunken. A world where even a swimming pool bloated the flat, level, concrete landscape. In need of a cement pond, we had a fondness for *The Beverly Hillbillies*—finding oil, getting rich, moving to Beverly Hills. We could both look down on them for their ignorance and appreciate the luxury of that scorn—we didn't have to be jealous, since it was just pretend. We could also enjoy the fantasy of getting rich quick and putting something over on The Man. Perhaps that was the key to the show's success—both fantasy fulfillment and mockery. In this case, The Man was Mr.

Drysdale, the bank president, and the stupidest person on the show. We could all agree on that.

The last time I saw Mr. Elias, shortly before they moved, he told me his oldest daughter had married a lawyer, so maybe his child-rearing strategy had paid off. Where would we even meet a lawyer unless we needed one to get us out of jail? Didn't the Monopoly card suffice for that? We had a bail bondsman nearby. But a lawyer? We saw them on TV, along with the "swimming pools, movie stars."

I don't know who owns the house now, but on Google Earth I can still see those hedges between the houses, growing out of control through the fence without my dad to hack them back.

POOL PARTY

WE, THE POOL-LESS, mooned in the street under the bright unshaded sun, waiting for someone somewhere to invite us to a pool party. Pool party! What an alliterative concept! I actually was invited to one when I graduated from St. Mark's at the end of eighth grade—Cindy Koslowski, who lived on the other side of the tracks from church, from school, further from Detroit. Cindy was my girlfriend for about as long as it took for a green light to turn red, which was long for eighth grade. It was cold and rainy that June afternoon, so all we could do was look at the pool from inside their dry garage and eat hot dogs grilled by her father under an umbrella. I ached for her, and I ached for her pool—both aches unrequited. We did play spin the bottle after it got dark, but it was small consolation watching other boys kiss her—I'd built Pool Party up into a New Year's Eve kind of celebration: throwing each other in the pool, eating special adult food, drinking secret adult drinks like in some old Elvis movie I'd seen on TV while sick from school one day. Maybe you had to be in Hawaii for that to happen. Pool/Party/Pool/Party/Pool/Party. Sigh.

POOL 3: THE un-ZANY ZELEWSKIS

WE SIMPLY CALLED Randy and Marty Zelewski "The Twins." We had no others. Those two never did anything separately, except practice piano. They were like twin Beaver Cleavers with glasses. We swam in their pool more than any other one. Their mother was a devout-Catholic June Cleaver, and their father was a lunch-bucket-carrying autoworker version of Ward.

They lived on Jarvis Street, on the next block, which seemed miles away to us. They could've had the pool for years and we might not have known about it, except we heard the rare sound of splashing and spotted it one hot summer while retrieving yet another errant ball from a backyard. We started riding our bikes over to the twins' house to call them out in our sing-song at the back door: "Ran-dee, Mar-tee." I imagine their mother, who loved music, cringed at our crude, off-key voices.

The lure of the pool worked to make us friends with those nearsighted brothers. They both loved and fought each other while we witnessed quietly, afraid to take sides. The rest of us could only admire their fratricidal fury. Their street was fluky, dominated by families of girls. The twins themselves had two sisters—much younger, as if it took years for their parents to recover from having twins.

The twins looked like Mr. Peabody (a dog) and Sherman (the boy the dog had adopted) from the *Mr. Peabody's Improbable History* cartoon with their thick oversized dark glasses. Peabody and Sherman went back in time with the Way Back machine to fix history. We often recited the show's famous catch-phrase, "Drizzle drazzle, drizzle, drone, time for this one to come home," though honestly none of us strayed far from home. The next subdivision seemed exotic enough.

Usually, one of the twins was practicing the piano in their basement when we showed up. They had a swimming pool and a piano when most of us had neither. We ran in fear of music lessons (electric guitar being the exception). Their mother was strict and firm like ours, but she was also a reader, a music lover, and an avid churchgoer. She attended 8:00 a.m. Mass every day throughout her long life. The boys' daily practice was timed out on a stovetop timer we could hear going off while waiting for them outside. They fought over who put in their bench time first. We could hear them whining at their mother, accusing each other of cheating the clock. We often wore our bathing suits beneath our cutoff jeans, just in case. If we showed up too early, Mrs. Twins-mother shooed us away with the flick of her sharp, Jesus-honed wrist. Anyone who had swallowed that many communion wafers was a force to be reckoned with. The piano lessons had been her idea; we weren't sure whose idea the pool was, though it must've been a relief to her for the boys to tire themselves out in the pool while she quietly read a book.

Their mother seemed like the opposite of Mrs. Romano— short, homely, pale in her house dress. Perhaps at some point, she and her husband donned their suits to take a quiet swim, but my imagination even now cannot take me there. They seemed older than our parents, already slumping from a lifetime of hard work and taking what was given. Their father pulled into the garage every day and took his lunchbox in the house, giving us a wave, which meant it was time for us to leave. We all ate dinner at the same time—factory time.

In defense of their stern mother, Marty went on to play keyboard in wedding bands throughout the tri-county area to supplement his meager income as a reporter covering high school sports for *The Macomb Daily*.

Legend had it that whenever they played at a wedding, the couple got divorced. Well, not quite a legend, but on those flat, cement streets, it didn't take much of a bump in the road to turn anything into myth. Truth is, they played at my brother's first wedding, and that one ended in divorce. Or, maybe the jinx was the hippie priest Father Frank, since he had presided over that wedding. Father Frank got high at the receptions and ended up marrying a classmate of mine, and that did indeed become legend. Marty and I spent one long afternoon in the pool in separate innertubes writing a book that was inevitably ruined when the ink got wet. Maybe this is a section of that book, still smelling of chlorine and adolescence.

None of us became good swimmers. We could not swim in those pools. We could stand up and bounce on our toes. Easy to keep our heads above water. Easier than it would be for the rest of our lives.

Years later, Marty showed up once in Pittsburgh with his wife, who I'd never met, for a weekend visit. He might've been more interested in seeing the city than in getting reconnected. Maybe he knew we took advantage of him back when they had the pool, and was slowly cashing in his chits, though most of our friends still lived in the Detroit area, so there couldn't have been a lot of cashing in. Maybe we were so used to being encircled that we hesitated to venture out toward any body of water too big to see across.

MIDDLE OF NOWHERE, NEW YORK STATE

ACTUALLY, WE ONCE swam in a built-in pool outside a motel in the Middle-of-Nowhere, New York, on our way home from visiting Aunt Barb and Uncle Jeb—I mean, Jack—in New Hampshire. We had never stayed at a motel before, much less one with a pool. An in-ground pool! With a diving board! A deep end! All of our fantasies come true at last. None of our pools had deep ends—four feet at the edges, maybe five feet in the middle—and certainly not the neck-breaker of a diving board. We didn't know how to dive, so it was all belly smackers and cannonballs. In between, we found time to dunk each other in the deep end. In my fantasy religion, baptism would be in a chlorine-filled pool. With the double sting of water smacking skin and chlorine, you'd know you were signing on to something serious. My father has fading photographic evidence of five children posing on that diving board, our lips a little blue, our eyes zombie-red—color film was unreliable back then. We looked like a colorized version of those pale British demon-children from *Children of the Damned*, the scariest movie I've ever seen—only the air conditioning kept me from walking out.

We had been headed home from a disastrous trip to New Hampshire to visit our uncle and aunt, the alcoholic twins. And their eight hysterical children. The disastrous parts do not involve swimming or pools. The visit left my parents so frazzled that on the way home they left the canvas house tent on the car-top carrier and splurged on that motel. I don't think they even realized initially that it had a pool, since it was in-ground, obscured from the road. Or perhaps they thought the pool was just another mirage in a lifetime full of them. My mother tried the old dodge of making us wait an hour after eating to avoid getting cramps and drowning, but we just skipped our usual dinner of five hundred peanut-butter-and-jelly sandwiches packed in the cooler and ran out the door and straight into the water. My eyes had never been so on fire before, red and stinging—Free Swim was nothing compared to the concentrated chlorine in that small noodle-shaped oval.

That night, the five of us slept on one double bed, and our parents slept on the other. We luxuriated in the extra space created by our competing brands of complete exhaustion.

BRIGHT IDEAS NEVER REALIZED

I'm trying to provide the voiceover for the group of boys growing up on Rome Street—my brothers, and all the others. I apologize to them for not being omniscient, or for being too omniscient. We never talked all that much. Our conversations were like clacking stones together to create some primitive rhythm. I suppose some tough guys thought their stones were bigger than everybody else's stones, but I think theirs were pretty much the same size. Apologies to Michel-Angelo. Sometimes we got ideas and strung out their fluffy clouds into thin wisps until they disappeared.

Once, we planned to walk across the Detroit River to Canada, to reach what we imagined was our closest body of water. The Detroit-Windsor Tunnel was out of the question. We thought the Ambassador Bridge was an option. Until we discovered it was illegal to walk across the bridge. I can imagine showing up at customs, the officer wanting to know if our mothers knew where we were.

One day, though, we did take a long walk in the other direction, down Dequindre Road to Universal City, the first and only mall in Warren, around five miles away. We were closer to a shopping mall than to any body of water. The mall's small fountain that smelled faintly of chlorine did not count. None of us purchased anything, though we did spend a lot of time in Spencer's Gifts, admiring the posters and incense, lava lamps, and raunchy jigsaw puzzles. The young cashier kept close watch on us, like a lifeguard at Free Swim.

While we failed to find a body of water, we did eat lunch at the Red Barn, one of the McDonald's copycat chains springing up across America. Had we ever even seen a red barn? And if we had, would there be a swimming hole nearby that wasn't covered in scummy green algae?

While seated in its orange plastic chairs welded to Formica tables, enjoying the novelty of eating in a restaurant, loading our French fries up with unlimited ketchup packets, we witnessed a young man pull out a gun. He was shouting—something about a girl. Was the girl in the Red Barn, up in the hayloft with another man? Chaos ensued. We were so jazzed by the excitement, the walk home seemed much shorter. No body of water, but we had seen a man with a gun as consolation. We were still thirsty.

NIGHT, SWIMMING, NIGHT

ON HOT, BRUTAL summer nights, there was no relief beyond sleeping on basement floors in sleeping bags. Or better yet, in backyards. Thus, the invention of the Sleepout, which released us from adult supervision. We'd set up a tent in someone's yard and spend the night. It had to be during an intense hot spell to get our parents to agree. The heat baked into the cement all day, then ganged up on us at night, radiating back up, offering no relief. Nothing to absorb it, take it in. I think our parents were relieved to escape the hot breath of our complaints.

Nobody had AC. Sleeping out was nearly equivalent to swimming in a pool in terms of out-of-body experiences. We snuck out of backyards and wandered in search of cool air, kings of the night on those empty streets. Quietly swaggering, loudly whispering. Smoking. Spitting. Drinking cheap wine when we were old enough to cadge somebody into buying for us outside a party store. Or, as we became more sophisticated, sneaking it into our paperboy saddle bags while somebody distracted Mr. Charlie, the clueless owner of Charlie's Market: Oh, Mr. Charlie, I'll just buy this candy bar to give me energy to deliver my papers!

One night, our brains reeling with mosquitoes, boredom, and desire, we concocted a scheme to go swimming in all three pools on the same night. The Triple Crown of Pools.

Like the walk to the river, this never happened. We talked a lot about doing a lot of things, and sometimes the talking was almost enough.

But I did do this one thing, alone. I went skinny-dipping in the Elias pool. Crazed by heat late on one those nights that never cooled down, I felt an inexplicable longing for a number of related things jumbling in my young mind, leading me out the side door of the house.

Sleeping in the basement, it was possible to slip out that door, particularly with the box fan rattling upstairs. If that night were a film, it'd be a silent film, since any sound might wake my parents or the neighbors. Outside, I could hear various fans swirling in the still air, the wishful thinking of those fans.

I'd slipped on my cut-offs—I didn't know where my bathing suit was, and I didn't want to wake my younger brother also sleeping down there—he might tell. Barefoot, I slipped out the door and around the house to the Elias's gate. I slowly opened it and tiptoed into their yard, the cool, damp grass pricking the bottoms of my feet. I don't remember a moon that night—I could have used its company—but with the streetlight glow from the front of our house, I made my way. I couldn't swim in my shorts and then drip down the steps back into the house, so I slipped them off. The ladder was flipped up into the safety position for the night. I pulled myself up over the edge of the pool and slid beneath the water like a sleek city-kid dolphin dude. My heart throbbed with internal moonbeams. I was hoping God was watching. I was at the age when I was always daring God to show up and see what I was doing. I wanted to get a rise out of him so he'd give life to the frozen church statues. I wanted him to take off the crown of thorns and let his hair down and walk on water. But, nothing doing.

I imagined the Elias sisters emerging from their locked house—no door closing, or footsteps—floating, really—into the pool with me, a thirteen-year-old boy, my voice hoarse with whispered changing. I had never even seen a live naked human girl. I thought if I touched one, she might evaporate entirely, as if her body was liquid, tenuous. But I imagined me and the Elias girls going in circles around the pool, creating a whirlpool so strong we could drift in circles for hours without consequence. That would have been enough for me, maybe too much.

Actually, I didn't spend much time in the pool, swimming back and forth across it under water just once, bumping my nose off the liner like a dolphin at SeaWorld, which was, of all places, in Ohio, far from any sea. I shivered with the heat of all I felt.

No one caught me, which left me feeling relieved, but wanting to do it again. No one would have believed me if I told them, so I didn't. Though part of me wanted to be able to deny that I'd done it. To be accused of having done it.

The day after my secret adventure, I went over to the twins' house to see if they wanted to shoot some hoops. Maybe what I wanted was to gloat—is that the word? To simply let them know that I had swam in that ordinary pool in the dark of night, and that I could never un-swim it. Like it was a secret partial-ownership, a kind of darkness time-share. We played Around the World, 21, and HORSE until we were all sweaty, then they asked me if I wanted to go swimming. I said, "No thanks." I'd been waiting my whole life to say "No thanks."

YOU CAN WAIT FOREVER for a happy ending. Or, redefine waiting. How do we distract ourselves while waiting is what we end up calling life. One day, I'll be walking in the dark and take a step and suddenly disappear into an in-ground swimming pool. Effortless, no ladder necessary. A kind of death—the heart-attack kind, not the cancer kind. The cancer kind is seeing the pool and trying to gauge the distance, to count the number of doctors and treatments standing between you and the inevitable pool. I'm not sure if it's an in-ground pool or above-ground pool or an actual natural body of water. But one day I will be certain.

I am hoping, I suppose, for the delicious shock of cold water. I am also hoping not to pee in the pool.

It would be easier to walk on water in an in-ground pool due to not needing a ladder. Due to the lack of the plastic bucket to clean your feet of the surrounding grass clippings and dirt before going up the steps. Due to the clear knowledge that you were attempting to walk on water.

If you are startled by the lack of solid ground beneath you, you will have a roadrunner's chance of continuing across. You laugh at the coyote scrambling to return to the cliff's edge—one of humanity's timeless images. I believe it's carved somewhere inside the Great Pyramids and the Not-so-Great Pyramids: the roadrunner, the coyote.

No one drowned in any of our pools, and maybe that's our miracle. They say you can drown in a teaspoon of water, but I'm guessing it's a tablespoon.

Is this all true? Could it be true, at least in spirit and longing? Or would the stinging truth of chlorine burn off my magnified memories? Here, I am left underwater again in my blurry pool of remembering, the cold silent rush of possibility, after midnight when the entire block calms itself to sleep under the melting wafer of our streetlight's moon dissolving under our tongues—the body of Christ, amen. I cannot swim far—despite my spreading of arms and legs, the stretch forward, the gliding kicks—without bumping up against the liner, but that too is its own comfort.

DOG/DOG

The Voice of Bugle Ann was the first book to make me cry—
Bugle Ann, a foxhound, died at the end, I think. I don't
remember anything about the book except being surprised
by my own tears. I might have been in fourth or fifth grade.
Perhaps that book's still out there making other kids cry.

When my daughter Rosalie was five, I took her to see *My
Dog Skip*, a film based on the memoirs of Willie Morris, the
writer and editor. In the dark theater, she burst into unrelenting
sobs when the boy struck his dog for not leaving the baseball
field. Some of the audience tittered at her sobs, though when
the dog actually died near the end, I heard numerous sniffles,
saw a lot of red eyes when the lights came up.

"Why did he have to hit the dog?" my daughter wailed.

"It's just a movie," was my lame response. She cried at the
right time—at the cruelty, not at the sentimental death.

I am trying to define cruelty. When there are no voices to
rise up and point fingers, we have to define it for ourselves.

I GAVE AWAY ANOTHER DOG. After swearing I would never do
it again. After writing a short story and screenplay called *No
Pets*, "inspired" by giving the first dog away. The first dog, Jake,
is long dead—I got him in 1977, gave him away in 1979. The
second, Jack, came along in 1990, so he's dead too. But he lived
a long, happy life getting spoiled by our old baby-sitter Jennifer.
If this were fiction, I'd change the names. Jake, Jack—a little

confusing. They looked nothing alike—Jake, a black and white springer spaniel mix with a cropped tail, and Jack, a golden retriever/lab mix, with a long furry tail—but sometimes they seem like the same dog. Dog, with a capital D.

With Jake, I was a twenty-year-old college student. Long hair and beard. Torn jeans. Pot smoker. Beer drinker. Jilted ex-boyfriend. With Jack, I was a thirty-six-year-old college professor. Homeowner. Short hair, sprinkled with gray. Mostly sober. Happily married.

How could I convince myself—twice—that I wanted, needed, a dog, only to fail both times?

I WAS OUT WALKING with my children Rosalie and Ramsey on a trail in Schenley Park, a large city park in my Pittsburgh neighborhood, when a big unleashed German shepherd came sprinting down a hill toward us. I grabbed a child in each arm and lifted. The dog jumped up against my chest. I struggled to hold both children above it. Some of the park dog people fight for the right to let their dogs run free to terrorize (or not) everyone else.

"Don't worry, he's friendly," a woman holding a leash cheerfully shouted down to me as she approached.

IN THE SIXTIES, collies were overbred because everybody wanted Lassie. A lot of them turned out not to be very nice dogs and ended up taking the Big Sleep down at the dog pound. After the various versions of *101 Dalmatians*, parents suddenly wanted Dalmatians for their kids. It happened after the release of the original cartoon in 1961, and it happened again with the release of the live-action remakes, *101* and *102 Dalmatians*. I suspect it's a completely new set of people each time. Nobody would be stupid enough to fall for the same thing twice. Would they?

You never see anybody cleaning up dog shit in any of those movies. In the film *No Pets*, I included a scene where the main character picks up crap with a shovel out in his yard to correct that omission, but nobody saw the movie, so I don't think we changed the world, but hey, somebody's gotta do it, even for Lassie.

Some of my most unpleasant memories of childhood are of my father's poop inspections in the yard. He worked for the Ford Motor Company at an axle plant. Long hours and little satisfaction. After work, at the supper table, he'd ask, "Did you clean up the dog crap today?"

I always said, "Yes," whether I'd done it or not. When he was in a particularly foul mood, he'd say, "Well, let's go out and take a look."

He'd go over that yard like he was looking for a leprechaun's pot of gold or a lost diamond ring. I'd be trailing behind him, cursing under my breath, our dog Prince following us, sniffing the ground, perhaps looking for a good place to make a new pile. My father always triumphantly located some stray petrified turd. He took incredible satisfaction in that, as if he'd found a concrete piece of all the verbal shit he took at work every day, a piece his son could scoop up with a shovel and dispose of.

Our yards are never clean, I'd tell my father now. There's always a little piece of shit out back, even if we don't have dogs. We can ignore it, pretend it doesn't exist. Until we step in it.

LARRY, A FRIEND of mine from college back in the seventies, had a dog named Zen, a big friendly black lab. When Larry graduated and was moving away, he let Zen out of his pickup truck in the woods and drove off, thinking that big dog could fend for himself, or that some farmer would stumble upon him and take him in. I think Larry must have been smoking too much dope. Now, that seems like an incredibly heartless thing to do. I guess back then, for Larry, it seemed like choosing freedom over confinement (the dog pound). We were all about freedom back then.

1977. THREE YEARS AFTER PRINCE, the idealized dog of my childhood, died, my girlfriend Debbie broke up with me. We'd gotten engaged in a desperate attempt to salvage our relationship, as if the ring could solidify what we could not. What did I do? I got a puppy. The idea of having pets appeals to our irrational side, the same side that makes us fall in love. And the same side that likes to be the boss, to control.

She was seeing someone else—a former friend who lived across the street from me. I attended Alma College, a small school in mid-Michigan—it seemed like everyone had known what was going on except me. I was living in a house off campus, and after the break-up I felt further isolated from the rest of the school. Humiliated. Hey, why not get a dog?

I circled an ad in the local paper and drove to a farm in the country in a terrible snowstorm to pick one out from the three remaining puppies. Snow swirled and drifted across those flat mid-Michigan roads. I had to park and walk the last quarter mile. The old farmer was in no mood for small talk as I stood over the box of puppies in the shelter of the barn. He seemed a little bewildered by what anyone was doing out in that storm. Some dumb college student feeling sorry for himself and looking for a quick fix, it turned out. I took the first puppy I picked up. That was the way I was then, clutching quickly to everything, not thinking. Out the barn door, the world was pure white. I cradled the puppy's pink belly against my own and trudged off into it.

When I was seven, my parents had given me Prince, a fat, brown mongrel—part beagle probably. He was already four years old. My older brothers were a year apart, and my younger brother and sister were a year apart. I was the middle child with a gap of years on either side. The dog was *mine*.

WHEN I WAS A TODDLER, my grandfather had given us, his five grandchildren, a "surprise" dog for Christmas. All I remember is that it chewed up my plastic fireman's hat. I was too young to understand, but I should have remembered the look in my mother's eyes when my grandfather walked in with that puppy Christmas morning. That *oh shit* look.

We didn't have that dog long enough for me to remember its name. My mother could not bear the added burden with my father working long hours, and none of us old enough to care for it. She stood in the driveway crying, explaining, as the man we called the dogcatcher took it away. She didn't even have a car to take him away in. We stood smearing the picture window with our blubbering as we watched old whatever-its-name-was being driven away.

I TOOK PRINCE FOR WALKS around the block, sometimes slipping the leash over the handlebars of my bike to let him pull me, some of the neighborhood kids running along, trying to keep up. In the heat of summer, he dug holes in the shade beside the house and lay in the cool dirt, panting and filthy. I told Prince my troubles and secrets, resting my head against his thick chest. I went to remedial speech class from kindergarten through eighth grade. It was enough for Prince to simply listen and sigh his long dog-sighs.

We had Prince for ten years, then one spring day my mother had him put down while I was at school. He had bad arthritis and could barely walk most mornings, particularly in that last long hard winter. We'd been giving him aspirin, mixing it in with his dog food. He slept next to my bed that last night. I think he knew. I know that sounds like typical dog-lover's mush, but I still believe it. He lay beside the low trundle bed, where I could reach my hand over and rest it on that solid bulk like it was a rock that would be there forever.

The day we had him put to sleep, I received notification in the mail of my first writing award, an honorable mention in the *Detroit News* Scholastic Press Writing Contest. I ran back to school to tell my writing teacher of the award. I was seventeen, and yes, I mourned Prince, but I was *seventeen*. I had a girlfriend, a car. I wanted to leave the house that still smelled of him and run toward something fresh—good news, the future.

My mother gave me his collar, and I removed his last dog tag with pliers and put it with the old ones that I'd saved. And the award letter—I saved that too.

I NAMED THE PUPPY JAKE, either after Jake Woods, the former Detroit Tigers second-baseman, or Jake Barnes, from *The Sun Also Rises*, my favorite Hemingway novel. It depended on who was asking and how I wanted to impress them.

Jake was six weeks old when I got him. I kept him in a box next to my bed and put an alarm clock wrapped in a blanket next to him because it was supposed to remind a puppy of its mother's heartbeat. I was trying to put some mileage between me and Debbie. My off-campus house was a hippie commune, and my housemates more or less embraced Jake, perhaps hoping I would stop moping around the house.

That time, it had been my idea to get a dog. An adult choice—a young adult choice. I thought it'd be cool to have a dog, an accessory to help define myself. And take my mind off Debbie. Hadn't I had another dog who'd made me less lonely and had helped me through rough times? But times were simpler back then, when I had to go in the house when the streetlights came on, and Prince was the one who wandered at night, not me. After I finally ended my self-pity party, I was the one who wandered while Jake was left home alone sulking in the tiny living room filled with record albums, plants, candles, and drug paraphernalia.

Once, while I was out, Jake chewed up albums by The Grateful Dead and Joni Mitchell that belonged to my housemates, and I had to buy replacements. The dog didn't understand why I stayed out all night, then hit him with a newspaper because he'd crapped on the floor. I didn't have much patience with anything in my young life, and one thing you need with a puppy is patience. I wanted everything right away—a new girlfriend, a quick high, whatever. And back at the house, I felt I was missing opportunities. I hung out at the Student Union on campus, drinking large cups of coffee and waiting for someone to sit down across from me and say hello. It wasn't enough to have Jake listen—I could no longer put myself back in a place where I could imagine him understanding.

In the dead of winter, that small house felt smaller. Staying home with Jake at night while I studied *was* often a comfort. He gave the house warmth—playful and rambunctious, chasing balls, knocking over books, wagging his stub of a tail. We were poor students and turned the thermostat down as far as it would go each night. Jake provided real warmth, curled up at the foot of my bed, and the illusion of stability.

WE USED TO TURN ON the porchlight and let Prince out to wander the streets in the evening. He'd usually come back in an hour or so, barking at the door to be let back in. The people who'd given him to us had let him out like that, and Prince expected it, so we naïvely went along with it. He was such a friendly dog, no one in the neighborhood complained—at least, to us. Sometimes he stayed out all night, and when he did show up again, he was extremely thirsty, lapping up bowls of water, then sleeping the whole next day. Once, he returned with his belly slit open. The wound required at least fifty black stitches, but the next night, he was pawing at the door, ready to go out. He liked to run free, and who could blame him. All the dog books talk about how your dog will be happier trained because it will know what to expect from you, what you expect of it. If you get a dog, I certainly believe you should train it properly. But happiness? I'm not sure.

Few people wandered the neighborhood streets after dark. Still, now it seems crazy and selfish that we let Prince out, imposing him on the neighborhood. When he got older and forgetful, he sometimes barked at various neighbors' doors instead of ours, and we'd have to go retrieve him. Once, a friend thought it was his dog barking and opened the door. Prince trotted in, quite content, and plopped down on their floor.

THAT FIRST WINTER WITH JAKE, it never stopped snowing, piling up layer upon layer in the yard. I spent a lot of time out in it, trying to potty-train Jake. He could barely jump over the accumulated snow to find a spot to go.

Whenever I spotted Debbie walking home with the Other Guy, I picked Jake up and hugged him close, though in truth he couldn't protect me from the huge heartache I felt in those moments.

Our yard was unfenced, so I let him out on a long chain attached to the wall near the back door. He invariably got tangled in the chain, and I'd have to go out and unravel the knots and pull him back in by the collar.

One night, Jake managed to slip off the chain. He was fast, and I quickly lost sight of him. I ran to my car, then drove the dark, snowy streets for hours looking for him, frantic and afraid for him out there alone. Finally, I gave up and drove home. When I pulled in the driveway, he was sitting in the snow waiting for me. My heart leaped—with relief more than joy. I should have known he'd return, as Prince always did. But I treated him so poorly, I imagined he might be consciously running away. All I had for him was a food bowl and a fifty-pound bag of Gravy Train.

Patty, my first girlfriend after the Big Break-Up, preferred to sleep on the floor with Jake. That should tell you more about me than Patty, an incredibly generous, compassionate woman who died in a car accident one year later.

THAT FIRST SUMMER after getting Jake, I went back to my parents' house outside Detroit. My father had gotten me a job in the Ford plant to earn tuition money. Jake had a fenced-in yard to roam in, and my mother and younger brother and sister to give him attention. I worked afternoons, 3-11, and often went out drinking after work. I slept in, hungover in the mornings, and sat on the porch squinting into the sun and patting Jake's head, waiting till it was time to drive to the plant again. I had enough energy to throw the ball when he brought it to me, but that was about it. My mother fed him while I was at work. The old dog-crap shovel was waiting for me, and that summer I picked up a lot of shit, just like the old days.

After my senior year, I worked in the factory again. I had been accepted to graduate school at Bowling Green State University for the following fall. When I drove down from Detroit to look for a place to live, I could not find an apartment that allowed dogs—though I only spent one day looking, then took an efficiency in a row of converted motel rooms. Jake would be a burden to me starting over alone in a new place. I knew I'd feel tied down. Knowing no one there, I didn't have a chance of finding a houseful of other people who didn't mind helping out with Jake. I wasn't settled enough, didn't want to be saddled. I drove back to Detroit and shrugged.

My parents agreed to keep Jake at home with them for the school year. I was supposed to find some friends and a house that allowed dogs for the following year, but at the end of that first one, I knew I didn't want him back. I was spending half my time in school, and the other half in bars. Neither allowed pets.

Jake wasn't even sure about me when I came home on breaks and long weekends. Who was his master now? He'd taken to sleeping in my sister's room, under her bed. Once I bent down to reach him under there, and he snarled. Jake was high-strung and protective. My coming and going messed him up. If he was my dog, why was I leaving all the time? It pains me to remember my selfishness, taking advantage of my parents, neglecting the only real, individual responsibility I had in life then. I loved to see his wagging butt at the gate as I pulled up in my old Plymouth. I always had a rawhide chew for him. Since all he had was the stub, he waved his whole butt as if to compensate. But the chew—that was hardly compensation.

I HAD RENTED A BIG FARMHOUSE with some friends for the following year. The lease said *No Pets*, but I doubt anyone would have bothered us out in the country if I'd taken Jake along. One of my housemates ended up getting a cat. I was twenty-three years old and couldn't imagine carrying a dog through the next ten uncertain years of my life. When it became clear that I wasn't going to be taking Jake back with me, my parents worked to find him a new home. My mother put an ad in the church paper. Jake had snapped at one of the neighborhood children, and my parents knew he wasn't getting the attention he needed and deserved.

An older couple answered the ad and took Jake that summer while I was away on a camping trip. My mother apologized for giving him away while I was gone, but I was relieved. I didn't want to have to face up to what I'd done. It was easy to just have him gone, no traces.

But then a couple of weeks later, the phone rang. It was the man who had taken Jake. My parents were on vacation, so I was watching the house. Some of my old high school buddies were over, drinking a few beers. The man and his wife had decided they couldn't handle Jake. He was too wild and not adapting well to living with them. They wanted to give him back.

I held my fingers in my other ear to hear above my friends' laughter. I swallowed hard. "No, I can't take him back," I said.

"You know what that means?" the man said.

"Yes. Yes, I know," I said, "But I can't take him back." I quickly hung up the heavy black telephone, my hands trembling. It meant they would be taking him to the pound.

I hope somebody picked him up, or that the couple gave him another chance and he ended up being a good dog for them. At that moment, I felt like I was letting Zen out of the pickup truck. I told no one about that phone call. I swore I'd never get another dog.

VIC, OUR NEXT-DOOR NEIGHBOR in Pittsburgh, got a puppy named Mutley shortly after my wife and I moved in, and before we had children or a dog of our own. Initially, I was excited to have a dog next door, to reach over the fence and pet him. I even bought a box of milk-bone treats. But Mutley soon became a nuisance. Victor and his wife at the time, Jennie, both worked full-time. They left Mutley on a short rope in the small gap between our houses, the area we called the Echo Chamber, since all the brick magnified any little sound. Mutley barked. And barked. And who wouldn't, stuck walking around in his own shit all day? After he snapped at my hand one day, I stopped giving him treats.

Vic and Jennie fought often. They had two small children. Once I heard Jennie call them "fucking misfits." We didn't borrow cups of sugar from them. I could easily imagine a feud developing to the point where we were the "fucking neighbors," so we filed anonymous complaints with animal control, who sent them warnings about nuisance animals. Mutley, for his part, chewed through the rope and escaped on more than one occasion. A huge, hairy dog, he looked like a mound of black, overgrown weeds. Part wolfhound, part buffalo. He once ran right into the busy street and got hit by a car, but kept on running. What could damage his brain more than the treatment he got? He never got walked. He never got petted. The children were afraid of Mutley and wouldn't go near him except to taunt him with sticks. In response to our complaints, they let him sleep in their basement. Don't ask me what pleasure they took in that dog. Don't ask me what pleasure ever went on in that house. When we returned from a year in Miami where I was a visiting professor, Mutley was gone, and so was Jennie. We never asked, and Vic never told.

VALENTINE'S DAY. KRISTIN CALLED ME at my office. She had a surprise for me. "Come home right away," she said. Like something couldn't wait—something alive, urgent, more than a gift to unwrap. "Denise's here." My heart sank, then bubbled back to the surface—I just knew it was a dog. Denise, her best friend, had recently gotten one herself.

All the way home, walking fast, half-running, my backpack bouncing off my shoulders, I hoped I was wrong. I did *not* want that burden again. But I opened the door to find little Jack on the kitchen floor, a refugee from the Animal Rescue League: thin and clumsy, his blond fur matted, dirty, and wild.

Work had been unbearable—back-stabbing viciousness, personal attacks, inter and intra-departmental battles. My credibility and integrity had been openly questioned at a department meeting by people I thought were friends. At a low point in my career, I dreaded every minute at work, every sleepless night. I used to call it "going to school," but it had become "going to work." I retreated into myself, driving Kristin crazy with long, sullen silences. She was desperate to pull me out of the funk, desperate enough to surprise me with a dog.

I stood stunned, speechless. "We can take him back," she kept saying, reading my concern. They had expected joyful surprise, but I'm sure I had that "oh shit" look on my face. I felt if she took him back, it would be a scar on our love that she had guessed so horribly wrong, that she didn't know me well enough. Poor Jack, his toes scrabbling over tile to greet me, looked pathetic. I couldn't imagine driving him back to the shelter.

It was my fault. I had often spoken of both my idealized love for Prince—the comfort dogs provided, the pure simple love— and of my guilty regrets about Jake, how not being mature enough to take good care of him was one of my big failures.

Kristin and Denise had gone to the shelter "just to look." Denise, single, living alone, had gotten her dog from the same place—a large, hyper dog who jumped on people and seemed out of control. Her dog annoyed me, and I thought it cruel to leave it locked up in her tiny apartment all day. Her dog reminded me of Jake. I wished Denise wasn't there. I needed to talk to Kristin alone. Already on tension overload, I was unprepared to even consider whether to keep him or not. "We can take him back." But I couldn't. Jack looked like how I felt. He needed a bath. So, we kept him.

Kristin, for her part, took him to a dog training course sponsored by the local community college. I had a class the same night, a convenient excuse. I still resented the implied responsibility, though she got Jack for a good reason—I needed an outlet for all that tension. Something simple to take care of, something which would love me unconditionally.

I refused to name him for a week—if he didn't have a name, maybe we could still take him back—but finally, as we sat with him on the floor at my in-laws the next weekend, I named him Jack—simple, unpretentious. At the time, I didn't think of the similarity to Jake, who might have still been alive then, if he hadn't been put to sleep ten years earlier at the pound.

I was 36 when Kristin brought Jack home and he became part of our lives. If we were going to have kids, it would have to be soon. Like many young couples, we'd been imagining we had forever to have kids. We'd agreed to do so someday, but the *somedays* in front of us were dwindling. We had decided to start trying the year Jack showed up. We seemed primed and ready to settle down, so maybe a dog could fit in nicely.

Taking Jack to the park across the street forced me into getting regular exercise. On the trails, under the veil of leafy green trees, we ran in sync down the clear paths. Good-natured, curious, and playful, he did indeed help me relax. He became house-trained fairly quickly, and because of my flexible work schedule, I was able to be home with him a good portion of the time.

But Jack wasn't enough to completely ease the stresses of work, and later that spring, I got the opportunity to be a visiting faculty member at a university in Florida the following school year. Kristin quickly flew down to look for a place to live and landed an exciting job herself. But what about Jack? Whether it's Bowling Green, Ohio, or Miami, Florida, finding an apartment that allows pets can be difficult, particularly when deep inside, you don't want to find that apartment. Jack had grown into a big, long-haired dog who needed to be outside, running around. He'd hate the heat, and the fleas in Florida were awful. In Pittsburgh, we had Schenley Park right across the street—where could we run him in the heat of congested Miami? I was ready again with my excuses not to be tied down while starting over some place new. Jack stayed with my in-laws in Pittsburgh. They did not know the Jake story, and willingly took him "for a year."

Kristin had to move to Miami early to start her job. *No Pets* was filmed in Pittsburgh that summer. We didn't talk about it much, except as a writing project. It wasn't *our* story—not yet. I stayed in Pittsburgh while we finished up filming. Before I left, I took Jack in to get him "fixed." Any animal taken from the shelter had to be neutered within six months. The timing was bad—three days before I left for Miami. When I brought him home from the clinic, he was groggy. When I put the enormous plastic collar around his neck to keep him away from the stitches, he kept bumping into things. He seemed terrified and confused, so I took it off. He slumped in the corner and slept. It was the humane thing to do, to keep dogs from procreating, keep more unwanted dogs out of the shelter, but as he lay there panting in the August heat, I just felt sorry for him. During the filming of the movie, actors reenacted the abandonment of Jake. And with Kristin gone, I had nothing at home to distract me from the fact that I was leaving another dog behind.

THE WEEK AFTER I dropped Jack off at Kristin's parents and headed south, he ripped the stuffing out of their couch cushions while alone in their house for the day.

In Miami, in a small unfurnished apartment, we were suddenly released from many of our adult burdens, not the least of which were the stresses of my job. As Visiting Faculty, I was everybody's friend because I was *just visiting!* Lots of parties, but no committee meetings. Soon, we had our old life back, and thoughts of Jack receded. Our in-laws called us to give updates and ask advice. My mother-in-law took him to the park near their house every day. At Christmas, we visited, and he seemed happy to see us. Then, we found out Kristin was pregnant.

ONE SUNDAY MORNING, I was reading the newspaper on our deck that overlooked a canal between two islands in the middle of Biscayne Bay. Our island of apartment buildings looked out onto the expansive yards of the luxury houses on the other island. I might have been a little hungover. Kristin wasn't pregnant then, and we still went out partying on weekends.

I heard some dogs barking, but that wasn't unusual. One of the homes behind us had a number of dogs. I also heard the sound of children playing—also normal, for another house had two or three young children. But the barking seemed more frenzied and persistent than usual. Then, I heard shouts. Then screams. I got up and looked across the canal, and there in the children's yard a black rottweiler named Dexter had a young girl's arm in its maw.

A group of people on a boat in the canal were shouting and pointing. The young girl's mother stood by her back door screaming. The child was also screaming. Dexter wasn't making a sound, his jaws clamped on the girl.

I dropped the newspaper and started running toward the bridge over the canal down the road. What was I going to do? I had no idea. I saw a patrol car and flagged it down to give directions to the house.

A policeman shot the dog, and an ambulance took the girl and her mother away. All afternoon, silence hung in the thick, humid Miami air. Dexter's owners' other dogs kept barking until someone yelled "Haven't we had enough of your dogs for one day?"

A door opened, and the other two dogs disappeared.

The voice was angry enough to pierce that thick air, carry down the canal what I think all the neighbors were feeling, our hearts feverish over what happened to that little girl. "Haven't we had enough of your dogs for one day?" Jack was 1,500 miles north, running in the snowy park with my mother-in-law and a neighbor's dog named Shadow. In Miami, I was sweating.

THAT SPRING, AFTER I was done teaching, we returned to Pittsburgh, and to Jack, and we fell into a relaxed routine with him over the summer. We prepared the house for the baby due in August, Jack happily padding under our feet.

When our son Ramsey was born August 21 and we brought him home from the hospital, Jack was curious. He showed no signs of jealousy, made no threatening moves toward the baby. He licked Ramsey's feet and tried to lick his face. Ramsey was so tiny, we were worried Jack would accidentally hurt him, but he was always gentle. As Ramsey learned to crawl, then walk, Jack became a steady, panting presence at his side. We were a family, the four of us. I tried to keep up our runs together in the park, but they were shorter and less frequent.

Then, Kristin became pregnant again, and when Ramsey was sixteen months old, Rosalie was born, January 12, 1995. We had two kids under two: often, Kristin and I were up with one or both of the kids during the night, our lives a blur of sleeplessness, fatigue. All our attention was focused on the children—on getting through each day, providing for them. Jack had to provide for himself. As we struggled through that first winter with both kids, I barely got Jack out across the bridge into the park, and I didn't take him down the trails, but limited him to walks around the small playground. I got behind on cleaning up the crap in our tiny backyard, piles of it out there, frozen in snow.

Pets can't object. They can't say, *Hey, take me for a walk. Hey, scratch my ear. Hey, it's not my fault, don't blame me.* What can they do? They can piss and shit on the floor, and that's what

Jack did. His "accidents" clearly were not accidents. He knew how to ask to go out. He hadn't had an accident in the house since before we'd left for Florida. We were so frazzled with the two babies that it took a while to 'listen' to his message. People often compare having a child to having a pet—both are commitments that tie you down. In other words, if you can't handle caring for a pet, you certainly aren't ready to be a parent. The big difference: you can give your dog away. Your children—your children are with you always. In Kristin's old high school, girls in health class had to carry around an egg for twenty-four hours without breaking it as a lesson about how much responsibility being a parent is. But if the egg was a pet, and the egg broke, you could just go out and get another egg.

Our baby-sitter Jennifer came two mornings a week to watch the kids while we worked upstairs—Kristin is a writer too. Jennifer loved Jack, and her family dog had recently died. She told us if we ever decided to give Jack away, to let her know. When Kristin brought it up, I refused to discuss it. Jack wouldn't have ever harmed the children. He never even remotely made one move that could be perceived as threatening. Jack was clearly unhappy, but what would it say about me if I gave another dog away? I didn't want to admit that failure again. It would seem selfish to give him away, yet wasn't I being selfish by keeping him? Or, even cruel? A lot of people either get dogs because they are *not* having kids, or *for* their kids. But if you get a dog for your kids, your kids should be old enough to help take care of the dog. Ask my father, Captain of the Poop Patrol.

I KEPT TRYING TO ARRANGE my priorities as we had first one child, then another—to give attention to my marriage, to my children. Kristin and I took care of the children all day, then collapsed into bed together with an exhausted kiss on the cheek before curling away from each other into sleep.

Despite Kristin's good intentions, getting me a dog didn't make my job any better—I couldn't take him into work and have him bite my enemies. And I had to find time to do my own writing amidst the chaos of our household. Kristin, for her part, was juggling two part-time jobs. And in the middle of this, our young dog was running around wondering *what about me?*

I loved Jack. In the park, I was drawn into his eagerness to smell everything in the big world, to explore, his bushy tail wagging. I loved reaching over the side of the bed where he slept on the floor, just to feel him there, his calm, heavy, rhythmic breathing. I loved to watch him swim, his head above the water, hurrying toward the stick, any stick. I miss him. I miss Jake. I miss Prince. I miss the idea, the *ideal* of having a dog.

Why didn't that love transfer to commitment, as it does for children? I am not that woman in the park who imagines letting her dog off the leash gives it its freedom, blind to how others are inconvenienced, threatened. And I'm not Victor, abusing my dog, then my children, then my wife. I know a lot of people with dogs. Some let them run loose. Some save their ashes, visit their cemetery plots. Some, like Jennifer, get a replacement dog after their previous dog dies. After her dog Waffle was hit by a car and killed, our neighbor across the street quickly went out and got an identical dog and named him Waffle. Not even Waffle II. Just Waffle.

WATCHING JACK MOPE around the house, it seemed like he was still wearing that stiff plastic collar the vet gave him—he couldn't get close to anything, to any of us. One morning, Kristin trudged down the stairs with Rosalie in her arms and stepped into a big pile of shit. That was it. I relented and agreed to give Jack to Jennifer.

Kristin insisted I take Ramsey, who was one-and-a-half, with me when I gave Jack to Jennifer. So he'd know where Jack was, that he had a good home. We packed up his toys and bowls, the leftover dog food, the leash, the pooper scooper. I strapped Ramsey in his car seat, let Jack in the other side, and drove off, numb with panic.

At Jennifer's, I led him into their house and unloaded the bags of dog things, holding Ramsey in one arm. They wanted me to take off my coat and stay, but I didn't know how long I could hold it together. I looked at Jack and said, "Be good." And stepped out the door. Then I turned to go back, to pat his trusting head one more time, but stopped myself and hurried down the steps.

After I strapped Ramsey back in the car. I stood in the street sobbing, saying, "What am I doing? What am I doing?" Ramsey sat quietly in his car seat, his big, round eyes taking it all in. Back home, his mother was breast-feeding Rosalie. What had I done? I had given another dog away. I got in the car and drove off.

A sequel to *No Pets?* One movie reviewer said she cried when the dog was given away. I tried to stick in a joke at the end of that scene to keep it from being sentimental. Sitting in the audience at the premiere, I wanted to hear more laughter than I did. Jack: part golden retriever, part lab. Every day was a bad haircut day for him, his long fur splaying in all directions. Bigger than Jake, huskier, stronger. I never gave Lassie away. Or Lady. Or Benji. I gave away real dogs.

JACK WAS EXTREMELY HAPPY with Jennifer, her mother, and her brother. He got gravy on his food every night. He ate two meals a day (plus the cat food he stole from their three cats). He gained weight, based on the studio photograph Jennifer sent us—she finished college and got a job as a dental hygienist. She always told us that we could visit Jack anytime, but I didn't have the heart for it. We still occasionally stumble onto a stray dog hair somewhere, and the rug where Jack had his accidents still smelled faintly for a time—some hot summer days, playing with the kids, bent down on the floor, I got a whiff. We'll never get rid of every single hair. They lurk under radiators, they've woven themselves into our rugs.

Yes, I gave two dogs away. I gave Jack away because we weren't doing right by him. Because we had a baby-sitter who loved him and made it easier for us. We had a very tiny yard. We had no time to walk him. Unhappy, he had accidents on the rug. See? I always have excuses. But what about that phone call, that brusque, cowardly response, turning my back on Jake, on my responsibility toward him? Would even our neighbor Victor have been that cold? How will I react when my children call, in some kind of trouble, asking for help?

Kristin asked, "Am I the bad guy in this story?"

"No," I told her. "I am."

Sometimes, thinking of the dogs, sadness swells up in me, and I feel like Bugle Ann just died. You can second-guess me, as I've second-guessed myself. You can blame me, as I blame myself. I am haunted by my dogs, and I will never get un-haunted. Two young, healthy dogs. Jake, Jack. Jack, Jake. I proofread for consistency of names. Jack? Jake? Jake? Jack? My dogs were not my own flesh and blood, and that's what allowed me to give them away. Photos bear witness, and the names are not forgotten. But if you called me on the old heavy black telephone, I would not take them back.

THE CHALLENGE
OF THE SUNRISE

Watching the sunrise on the east coast is harder than watching the sunset on the west coast. Ask what's-her-name.

My younger brother and I camped at a Massachusetts state park in our father's old canvas house tent that smelled like musty childhood. We had escaped a Detroit summer of factory work and ran off with the tent, two sleeping bags, and a baggie full of dope.

A young schoolteacher camped alone at the next site. We invited her to our fire. Drinking and smoking, we sat on fold-out campstools we'd lifted from the garage back home. Our father, mad at us for leaving factory money on the table, but nostalgic for his own reckless pre-factory memories, gave us his retroactive blessing.

Here, imagine small talk. Very small. Stoned small talk. My brother and I hardly talked to anyone all summer. Seven-day work weeks, racking up future tuition money. Our lips smacked softly off beer bottles, oiling what had rusted. No singing around our campfire. We listened to waves crash through trees.

The campfire started out as a perfect asterisk and then crumbled into disoriented ashes, and from then on, we just tossed on logs, hoping they'd catch eventually. We squinted through the smoke at each other.

Using that theory, imagine me and her suddenly in her orange nylon tent. Imagine my brother's head shaking warily through the flames as we wandered away into a movie he'd seen before. Was he content to tend the fire alone? You'd have to ask him.

Her tent was tiny. I keep typing tent as tend. I tend to do that—tired, stoned, crumbling into ash. But not too tiny. We had sex. Small sex that didn't yank up stakes like a good storm. A breeze through the trees cooled the hot tent. The campground fell into waves of silence. Night bugs played tiny acoustic guitars. The glow of light outside the wooden bathhouse, civilized in the distance. Now what?

Sleep was out of the question, and so was my leaving. The answer was to watch the sun rise over the ocean. We'd both seen it on postcards and agreed it might be worth it, perhaps better without the gloss.

I was not a schoolteacher camping alone. I was studying drug intake at a small college up north. My brother was doing the same at a larger state college further north. We were both in a state. We imagined we were escaping our future, putting one over on the Big Foreman in the sky. Did you ever have a foreman?

As we watched the sunrise, I took a photo of her from behind with my 110 camera. You can imagine how that came out. But I'll tell you: blocking the sun, her rumpled sleepless body in silhouette was outlined by the Big Spotlight. I almost wrote beautiful body, but that would be cheating. Like saying the sex was good and that we would keep in touch. Send each other postcards of sunrises for the rest of our lives.

In the morning, I fell back into gritty sleep in the house tent. My brother had made cowboy coffee and was smoking a morning doobie. I waved to him as I zippered up the rest of my life.

She was gone when I arose from the dead, having beat me to that daily miracle. Headed down the coast on her long solo summer expedition. Would she ever stay up all night to see the sunrise again? Not if it meant spending the night with a stoned factory rat from Detroit who couldn't remember her name.

Not saying she could remember mine. Or wanted to. I think she might be happy with the way the photo came out. A dark, anonymous blur looking away from me and toward the sun.

On the California coast, you can just say, hey, let's walk down to the beach to watch the sunset drop its ball into oblivion. Afterwards, you walk back to wherever and get on with the night, checking your watch, going to sleep whenever you damn well feel like it, satisfied that it's over, with its delicious disappointment. I've seen more than a few sunsets. None has cost me more than a parking ticket.

I think disappearance is easier than arrival. Some think the opposite. What was the beach song that summer? Hum me a few bars and see if I can guess it. Not Barry Manilow!

You can spend your whole life searching for delicious disappointment. I can't say how delicious or disappointing it might be, having given up on that. Having taken down the house tent with my brother after evacuating the ghosts of our parents and siblings. It's a two-person job to remove the center pole without everything collapsing on you.

We split the driving on the way home, as we always did. In our familiar brotherly silence. Stuck with Barry Manilow on an AM radio. My brother knew better than to ask how it was. I knew better than to tell him.

Last week, he called from California to mention he had no pictures from that trip. I said I'd send a few. I paused, but I did not send him the sunrise. All these years later, it still felt like a violation of a silent pact I'd made with her. An unspoken agreement that we were human and both needed that human thing.

After the sun rose clear and unmistakably up, we walked back to the campground holding hands. Then we stopped to look at each other and held both hands as if in some ritual ceremony. Then we let go. Worth it to have five seconds of holding two hands. But I've never been able to do it again.

DROUGHT

To Rochegude and back from the small village of Laval-Saint-Roman is my favorite bike ride in France. On small un-trafficked roads that are hilly but not mountainous, cutting through vineyards and the occasional field of sunflowers or lavender, I can disappear into the rhythm and simplicity and feel embraced by the landscape. It is rare that I have to click my cycling shoes out of the pedals and stop for anything.

But I always stop for coffee in Rochegude at the Café du Course—I call it the Rock and Roll Café, the walls crowded with large, tacky paintings of old rock stars, one after another. Given the nature of rock stars, I have to look closely to be sure who some of them are—Bowie or Iggy? Madonna or Lady Gaga? Dylan (definitely), Marley (definitely), Jagger, or Steven Tyler? Prince, or Little Richard? It's like I'm at a concert, stoned, squinting from the cheap seats. I appreciate the possibilities, the lack of certainty. I add a sugar cube to my coffee and stir.

It looks like the place—a bar/restaurant/café—is hopping at night, given the indoor and outdoor seating, the ambitious dinner menu, the strings of colored lights. Though I am never here at night. I sit alone at the bar. They are often finishing the cleaning from last night, airing out the place, the small staff looking a bit hungover themselves. A young tattooed woman serves me a coffee while taking one herself. Sometimes, we flirt a bit, but that too is lazy. My French barely adequate, but she seems not to care where I'm from. I like that too.

In the tiny bathroom, the red urinal resembles the Rolling Stones mouth, their trademark. It's like a small altar—I clack up the three steps in my biking shoes. I always use the bathroom to save me peeing by the side of the road, though to be honest, the French don't seem to take notice one way or the other. I always exchange glances with the rock stars on my way back to the toilets.

IF YOU'RE WONDERING where I do come from, that would be Detroit, Michigan. How I got here is a long, long story, and it doesn't even make sense to me. It's like I'm standing on the table of southern France, and the four legs of that table just get wobblier whenever I try to explain. I am too old for the bartender. Any bartender. Too old to be riding my bike the fifty miles roundtrip, my wife Kristin would tell you. Thus, the coffee. Thus, the harmless flirting.

ROCHEGUDE, A SMALL VILLAGE on the edge of the pre-Alps, is dominated by an old chateau at the top which is in a constant state of renovation that shows little progress to my naked eye. I suppose I take comfort in that, imagining my own life to be in constant, but very slow, renovation. The castle is smaller than the church, which is rare in any village that has a castle. It's the perfect distance from my smaller village, further into Middle of Nowhere, France. I ride there, have a coffee, ride home.

Laval-Saint-Roman doesn't even have a café. It's what they call a dead village. Even the church is not in regular use. I have a small house nearby. I have a small water leak at the moment, but it's my problem. Well—it's now my problem and the village's problem, since it hasn't rained in six weeks. The mayor checked in to make sure I was not filling a swimming pool or watering my fallow fields. I just pointed to the rock-hard brown grass, and she nodded and drove away.

SOME DAYS, I IMAGINE my village is some post-apocalyptic landscape that somehow missed the nuclear storm that destroyed the
rest of the world. In the drought, it seems even more desolate
than usual. It might be the perfect place to live out my days.
Or, the worst place imaginable. I am hoping to figure that out
before my days are over. In the meantime, I am the American
loner with the horrible accent and the beautiful, outgoing wife
who speaks impeccable French.

ANOTHER REASON I AM DRAWN to Rochegude is that one late
morning, looping up onto the high road out of the village
that looks down onto the terraces and yards of a small cluster
of homes, I saw a man and woman making love on a beach
recliner on the pale gray cement of their patio. I like to revisit
that memory in person from time to time.

I wasn't sure at first—two pale, distant figures—but when
they came into focus, she was sprawled on her hands and knees
and he was pushing slowly into her from behind. They seemed
in no hurry—I saw no urgency whatsoever, no speeding up,
no slowing down, his hands on her hips as he eased forward
and she eased back. The sun lit them at a gentle angle, curling
beneath the porch roof. The church bells rang.

Hmm, I said aloud, then stretched that into humming as
I slowed to coast above them, then glanced back again to be
sure. I thought to stop but did not stop. He had a little belly
on him, and so did she. He was balding, the top of his head
shining in the sunlight. They were letting it all hang out, as we
used to say back in Alma, Michigan, back in the 70s, in the
house I lived in with four or five others, depending on who was
sleeping with you. It was all fluid until we ran out of water. I'm
not sure that metaphor makes sense, really, but in this drought,
all roads lead to water, or the lack thereof. I'm thinking about
unbridled thirst, and a total lack of self-consciousness, reveling
in instinct, giving in to the loosened reins of the times.

LIVING IN THAT OLD HOUSE were the best years of my young life. We were all students, and we were in no hurry not to be. Over Christmas break, Patty, who I was sleeping with off and on—off when we went on break, but I believe we were headed toward on again—was sleeping in the backseat of her cousin's car in Colorado when it skidded on the icy road and into oncoming traffic.

PATTY AND I USED TO FILL UP jugs with cold, metallic spring water out near Elwell, Michigan. A pipe rose up from the ground in the middle of nowhere. I keep saying in the middle of nowhere. Welcome to Nowhere, Michigan, population depending, give or take a few. Wherever Patty was, it was somewhere.

I did not attend her funeral, blaming it on the rituals of church, knowing Patty was an unbeliever like me, knowing I couldn't bear grieving in that public spotlight. When someone young dies suddenly, it's like the funeral director stabs you with a knife as you walk in the door. Stabs everyone. The weeping, the howling, the physical pain of grieving. *Fuck that*, I said, because it was easier. I hid in my dark room and wept.

I LIKE THAT THE WAITRESS seems to know me, the familiarity in that country where familiarity does not often come easy. She starts my coffee as I start clacking those plastic shoes across the floor. I know how much change to put on the bar, and she knows she does not have to count it.

In the café hangs a painting of a naked woman. Unlike the others, it's behind the bar. It has plenty of its own space, compared to the rock stars. Like a religious shrine. Mick Jagger, is her name Angie? I got up the courage to ask the waitress who was the model for the painting, and she said "my mother" and laughed. And I laughed.

I doubt she was telling the truth, but I like not knowing for sure.

DYING IS THE WORST DROUGHT. All our mouths at Alma went dry in the heat of that loss. Our mouths nearly caught fire with grief. Her best friend Lisa lived in our house. I remember how shocked she was to see Patty come out of my bedroom the morning after we'd slept together for the first time. Lisa acted like we'd both betrayed her. So, when Patty died, it was like/it was like/it was like—every record in that house, and we had a lot of them then, began skipping. Everything we said to each other had the abrupt jump of a record's skip. Lisa called me a coward/coward/coward.

I COULDN'T KEEP UP with Patty, which may have been the problem that turned us off then on again. She had a hunger, a craving. She dove headfirst into life while I was content to doggy paddle. The plastic milk jugs we'd filled with spring water filled up the backseat. She took a final swig direct from the pipe, then kissed me with it. If I had a picture of her, it would show her wet grin as she turned to pull me to her. It would be the picture above my memory-bar.

We found a spot further off the road in a small grove of pine trees. She lifted her long peasant skirt.

AFTER I SAW THE COUPLE, I thought to stop but did not stop. I knew I needed to keep going. Knowing you need to keep going is very different from keeping going. I love biking for the endless near-silence of it. The rhythm and repetition. The solitary journey. I like that my shoes click into the pedals and that I and the bike become one. As long as I keep pedaling.

I like going slow enough that it's safe to be doing one thing and looking around at something else at the same time.

THE CAST OF CHARACTERS from the rest of my life are waiting outside for the doors to open so that they can come in and get the best seats, or stand for the entire thing, depending—though

I am no rock star. I'm just saying I had a life between then and now.

But on that one voyeuristic day, I didn't feel that I did. Everything in between got flattened and sunk below the horizon. Patty dying, then me in France. Having sex outdoors. Quenching that thirst.

THE LAST TIME I saw Patty, she gave me back a few albums she'd borrowed. You don't have to do that, I told her.

She said, Oh, you never know.

I like that we never know. I don't like that we never know. I wish she would have kept them.

THE OTHER THING.

The other thing she gave me was an egg in which she'd made a tiny pinhole. She knew how to blow out eggs, then decorate them for Easter. The egg was not decorated. Or, the shell was its own decoration, the fragility of it. She had rolled up a tiny piece of paper very, very tightly and inserted it into the hole in the egg.

She told me there was a message inside it, and that one day when it felt right, she would tell me to break the egg and read the message.

THINKING, OR NOT THINKING, when we were off, not on, I threw the egg into an empty freight car passing slowly through town, part of the morning train that sometimes woke us up near the house where we'd slept together. Off and on.

A train, she'd whisper in my ear. Or, I'd whisper in her ear.

Sometimes we'd walk the tracks to school in parallel lines.

I LIKE AND DON'T LIKE that I'll never know what she wrote in that egg.

It'd be crazy to say she resembled the naked woman in the painting in the Rock and Roll Café. Long blonde hair, that's about it. I have no picture of her, clothed or naked. She was the artist, not me. And we thought we'd live forever, so who needed to take photographs. That was something our parents did.

I IMAGINE THE TATTOOED woman's husband runs the place. Maybe I'm imagining she flirts with me, an American cyclist with white hair and a gaunt face. She opens the place up, and her husband closes it.

I've been dreaming of symmetry my whole life, so I imagine it in many places of imbalance.

In other words, every time I ride that road winding out of Rochegude, I look down into that yard, imagining I might see them again. Imagining that they are still coming, coming, slow, steady.

THE FAMILY CALENDAR

For many years, my wife Kristin and I made a calendar for my family, choosing pictures from a selection sent in by my brothers and sister, my parents, and Elaine, my father's cousin. We marked birthdays, anniversaries, special family events, and selected the appropriate icons—birthday cakes, champagne glasses, balloons.

Elaine, an only child with an only child, had few relatives, so we drew her into our family. We celebrated her birthday—March 18. One Christmas Eve, she died of stomach cancer. We had known she was going—she knew too. In early December that year, as we put the next year's calendar together, we faced a dilemma: where to put Elaine?

During the first six years of calendars, we hadn't lost anybody. Each year had brought just happy additions, most recently, our daughter Rosalie. Then, suddenly, we had to mark a different kind of event for which we had no icon.

Elaine was the first to send her pictures in—they arrived in August, long before we'd even thought about next year's calendar. She was getting chemotherapy at the time, coping with nausea and weakness and fear. She sent a number of old extended family Christmas photos, along with a recent one of her in a luxurious dress she wore to a benefit ball at Somerset Mall—the fanciest mall in the Detroit area. She'd lost weight due to the chemo, so she had bought the new fancy dress just for the occasion. A friend of hers had bought her a ticket, knowing how few opportunities Elaine had to dress up. Knowing she was dying. For a while, it didn't look like she'd be healthy enough to even go to the ball, but she lasted to midnight. She stood alone in the photo, as she had much of her life. Along with the pictures, she sent a note: "All my hair's fallen out, so I'm old baldy now, but I've got a fancy wig!!"

Two exclamation points. That was how Elaine lived her life, even when everyone else was giving her question marks, ellipses. She didn't have many family photos because for a long time, it was just her and Bill, her son. She raised him by herself in the projects in Detroit. Her husband had abandoned them both.

The first real grief I ever saw was Bill's. He occasionally spent the weekend with us to give his mother a break. He was years older than me and my brothers and sister, and we admired him as a huge, invincible force. He was always big—tall and husky—like his mother. But one Saturday morning, I came out of the boys' bedroom to find him in my father's arms as he bawled, pure weeping, over a family he didn't have.

In October of the year she died, Elaine asked me if I knew of any good Catholic cemeteries. My only experience had been as an altar boy many, many years ago.

I told her about riding with the priests in the limo with E. J. Mandziuk, the funeral director—his stinky cigars, how they nauseated me. How afterwards, the priests usually slipped us some money. We used to get out of school, too. We went to either White Chapel or the one out by city airport, Mount Something-or-other. They both had a lot of grass—well maintained. I wanted to keep our conversation on the surface, moving—as far from the black earth underneath that impossibly green grass as I could. I went on and on, and she just let me. Finally, I just shrugged. She shrugged back and laughed, like she always did. What makes a good cemetery anyway? I don't think either of us knew.

WHERE TO PUT ELAINE in the calendar, when we knew she wouldn't live out the year?

Kristin suggested putting her on the cover. It had so far been reserved for grandchildren, and enough new ones had come along to make that an easy choice. But we were done with that. Rosalie would be the last grandchild.

"That's pretty maudlin, don't you think?" I said. *Here, Elaine, you're dying, so you get to be on the cover.*

"But if we put her inside, won't it just make everybody sad, having to see her picture every day for a month if she's already dead?"

"If we put her in the early months, maybe she'll still be alive."

We had to put her somewhere. We had her photographs, and we loved her. Finally, we put her in January, holding Rosalie, (whose birthday was January 12). and in March, in honor of her own birthday, wearing the Cinderella dress she'd be buried in.

She didn't live to see the calendar. My mother gave it to Bill after the funeral. We're the only family he had left.

KRISTIN AND I RECENTLY downsized to a condominium, taking a hard look at what to take with us. I went through all of our old photo albums, downsizing them too. We kept the calendars. I think we stopped doing them when everything went digital and we could just attach photos to emails and share them with one click. My father, age 95, never learned to use a computer. We celebrated his 95th birthday last month. Though he quit taking pictures a long time ago, he wanted my sister to print some up from the party for him. He has become an aficionado of large calendars with big squares. They help keep his memory alive. He attached some of those photos to it, making his own family calendar.

In the condo, tossing pictures from all the albums, I got distracted by the stack of calendars, looking at the photo of Elaine holding Rosalie on her lap and reading her a book. I remember celebrating Rosalie's birthday that year. Despite our fears, it was a comfort to see Elaine there with Rosalie all January. That photo is next to one of my mother holding Rosalie. My mother died two years ago, legally blind, wheelchair bound, and losing her mind. I remember thoughtlessly bringing pictures of our children to show her at a point where she was relying more on voices than faces to identify people.

Calendars mark our days, the small boxes of our lives, one after another. There were more pictures of Rosalie in the calendar than anyone else. Editor's privilege.

Elaine never had much. She worked for 20th Century Fox until her retirement. At the end, she faded quickly, so that the money she'd saved to die at home didn't run out. Hospice stayed with her. Dying at home was her only wish. Her home was a tiny apartment in a big complex a short bus ride to the nearest mall. Elaine had never been able to afford a car.

She was a large, busty woman with a big head of curly blonde hair. I imagine her firmly planted on the sidewalk, waiting for her bus. No giggle, no titter. She offered instead the solid fullness of her laugh. And it drew people to her. You felt safe around that laugh.

Elaine loved dressing up and going out. She liked highballs and the flash of costume jewelry. My mother told me they were suggesting donations to hospice instead of flowers at the funeral. I didn't go against my mother's wishes very often, but I couldn't picture the empty room, her casket unadorned—a jacket without a big gold brooch on the lapel. I sent flowers.

What can I say about Elaine to make her alive for you? To keep you from being as bored as you would be looking through my family calendar, crossing off the days?

IN ITALIAN CEMETERIES, gravestones include a photo of the dead. When I lived in Torre Gentile on sabbatical back in 1989, my biggest fear was that someone I loved would die while I was so far away. I didn't have a phone, and could only be reached by mail. It was the way I wanted it, but *what if, what if?* I often visited the village cemetery at the top of a nearby hill, staring at the small circles of glass enclosing the photographs of people I didn't know. Seeing them healthy and happy, I could imagine the little village peopled by those faces, the cemetery a village itself.

Once, a grieving family piled slowly out of a dusty, beat-up car. It hadn't rained in months, and their black dresses dragging over the path into the cemetery became dusted with pale dirt. I panicked as they approached, trapped within the stone walls. The oldest woman wailed in grief. I quickly squeezed out the gate past them, head down. There's no practice for this. I could imagine a late-night phone call, but I couldn't answer it.

That January, we traveled to France on my first sabbatical since the Italy trip. I had thought that Elaine would die while we were there, but right before we left, Christmas morning, my mother called with the news. We had a phone in France. We had two young children. We needed to be in touch. In case.

ELAINE GAVE ME my first drink when I was a teenager. She poured a little booze in my eggnog, winking at me while my parents sat in the other room. We visited her small apartment in Parkside Projects every Christmas, the seven of us sprawled over the ragged furniture stuffed into her tiny living room.

Sometimes I drove Elaine home from my parents' house after a family gathering. She was quiet during those rides through the dark—shy almost. *Thanks for the ride, Jimmy.* Then, out the door, waving from the entrance to her apartment as I drove away.

She doted on my children, on all children. They made her laugh her cartoon laugh. You never knew when she really thought something was funny. She was often the last one laughing, and you could hear something in that.

I TRY TO KEEP IN TOUCH with people from my past, and I feel a small death when someone completely disappears. Where are they? What are they doing out there somewhere? Do they ever think of me? I've searched for a way to both hold on and let go, but downsizing made me let go of a lot. Old clothes that were out of fashion or no longer fit—kept in my closet just to know where they were, even though I never wore them—had to go.

Not letting go kept me in protracted breakups that stretched over years. There never seemed to be a final goodbye, always one more phone call—maybe a birthday, maybe no occasion at all. *Just to check in, see how you're doing.* Then, *why not stop by sometime?* One year at Christmas when I was back in Detroit, I visited an old girlfriend from high school. We sat kissing on her couch. Then suddenly she pulled me to my feet. "You'll have to leave. My boyfriend is coming back. He lives here with me." I didn't blame her for not telling me earlier. She wanted to hold on, too, for a few minutes.

WHEN MY BROTHER'S MARRIAGE was falling apart, we kept their wedding anniversary on the calendar, though we knew they weren't going to make it to May 30.

That's gone from the calendar now, along with his ex-wife's birthday, June 27. It felt a bit harsh deleting her little balloons, but he's remarried now, and his new wife would not appreciate it. They'd been married fifteen years, so it really felt like we *lost* her.

MY GRANDFATHER lived until age 95. Every time I visited, I thought it might be the last time, but our goodbyes were casual nevertheless. When we were kids, he always stood on the porch or at the door, waving till we were out of sight, and he still did that, till the very end. I like the illusion of him waving there forever. Maybe eternal life is like that.

THE LAST TIME I saw Elaine, I knew it was the last. I hugged her an extra-long while, taking in the heavy perfume. She had lost over 50 pounds, and I was startled by how little was there. When someone has terminal cancer, you can't say, *I hope you're better soon.* I was trying to be so careful, all I could finally manage was, "Take care."

My father was dropping Elaine off on the way home. I was behind him in my car with Kristin and the kids. My headlights lit up his van, and I could see Elaine's golden wig glowing. When they turned off the main road, I wanted to follow, to keep her in light, but they disappeared in darkness.

THE NEXT YEAR, we had no new pictures, and Elaine got left off the calendar. We try to let go of the old in order to welcome the new—isn't that idea of the calendar, starting January 1? Will we ever get it right? I should have told Elaine about those cemeteries in Italy. Looking at her picture on the calendar from 1997 is like having Elaine's photo under glass. I can touch her face while she holds my daughter.

We imagined we would always keep the calendar going, the annual Christmas ritual of everyone opening their calendar at the same time. But we don't all even see each other at Christmas anymore. We're spread out across the country—my brothers, my sister, my father. The calendar reminded us that we are a family, but the definitions, the boundaries, keep shifting. Is it blood, is it legal contracts that bind us? My brother's second wife's children from her first marriage have children now, and I've yet to meet them.

My brother Tim and his wife in California are childless, separated from us by long, expensive flights. Despite occasional long-distance phone calls, it can be a challenge to keep them in the family orbit. The last year we did the calendar, he sent four pictures at the last minute, and two were blurry. I shared a room with him for over twenty years, and shared a lot of secrets. I will always love him. My own children barely know him.

MY MOTHER WAS with Elaine when she died. She and Elaine had gotten quite close. My mother's health was not good, even then. Elaine didn't care what readings were chosen for her funeral, what the songs were, so my mother used ones she'd already selected for her own funeral. She wanted to try them out, see how they sounded, and she knew Elaine wouldn't mind.

I missed Elaine's funeral. I didn't miss my mother's.

WE RETURNED FROM France at the end of April that year. My grandfather died in June. My mother had called one Sunday. "Grandpa isn't going to last much longer. He's stopped eating."

My mother, a nurse, knew when people were giving up.

"Okay," I said, swallowing hard. "I'll try to get home next week."

"He might not last that long," she said.

"I'll get home," I said.

That night while lying in bed, I realized I'd been cold on the phone, almost irritated by the inconvenience, the marring of my personal calendar. I got up and looked at the calendar in the kitchen's yellow light while Kristin and the kids slept above me. I had a softball game Monday night. I would go home Tuesday.

We lost the game. The next morning, as I poured coffee in my thermos for the drive, my father called. My grandfather had died in the night. He would have been 96 years old on June 25. In his calendar picture, he too is holding Rosalie on his lap. *Is* holding? *Was* holding? *Will always* hold?

SEPTEMBER NOW. September 22. Officially autumn. I'll turn on the furnace tonight. I'd hesitated the night before, holding out for one more night in hopes of another Indian Summer night. No such luck. I woke up with the sniffles.

I should know better. The stripping of the trees. The bare facts. When I was growing up, my other grandmother lived with us for fifteen years. I used to close the bedroom door a certain way in order to hear a distinct click. I believed that click kept her alive.

THAT DINNER AT MY SISTER'S—it didn't have to be the last time I saw Elaine, either. I could have seen both her and my grandfather again before they died. Calling it fear is not enough. My life's calendar in front, all those clean, blank squares; behind, the X's of disappointment, the question marks of the unresolved.

Kristin and Rosalie were both sick. We were supposed to go to Detroit for our family Christmas visit before leaving for France on New Year's Day, a departure imprinted on the new calendar we were giving out as presents. I decided to take Ramsey myself for a quick visit home to exchange presents. It would be at least four months before we'd be seeing family again; the only Christmas I'd ever missed was the year Rosalie was born.

Ramsey and I sat in my parents' crowded living room. Wrapping paper tore across laughter and surprise as we had an early Christmas with my siblings and their children, adults and children sprawled over the floor, sitting on each other's laps, cameras flashing and whirring while a hospice worker sat with Elaine in her silent apartment. My mother had just come back from visiting her. She slipped into a hard-backed dining room chair next to the couch where I sat holding Ramsey.

"How's she doing?" I asked.

"I'm not sure she knows who I am anymore. She won't make it till the new year."

Elaine's calendar sat at my feet in bright wrapping paper, stacked with the others. I handed them out all at once for the ritual unveiling. Who got the cover spot? My nephew Matthew, the first grandchild graduating from high school, a new landmark to celebrate. Elaine's calendar sat, almost hidden beneath scattered wrapping paper. I gently pushed it under the couch so it would not get buried. Or, just a little buried.

"Do you think I should go see her?" I asked my mother. Before she could answer, I asked, "Do you think it would make any difference to her?"

She knew I did not want to go. Elaine's position on the edge of our family blurred the lines of responsibility and love. "No, I don't think it would," she said. "If you go, it should be for yourself, not for her."

Ramsey was opening his presents, giggling madly among his cousins on the floor. The next day was Christmas Eve. We would be driving back to Pittsburgh to spend Christmas Day as a family—Kristin, Rosalie, me, Ramsey—just us.

I TALKED TO RAMSEY about my grandfather's death. He was nearly five. I had told him not to say, "I wish you would die." Then one day, he said, "Sky rhymes with die. You can say die if you're rhyming it with sky." And I said, "Yes, you can."

We did not take the kids to church, though we frequently debated it. Heaven and hell seem like fairy tales to us, but the temptation of a heaven was, and is, very real—so that the children, in the happy buzz of family life, could imagine it continuing forever.

I'm sitting here with that old calendar next to me, looking at December. I made a mistake. Elaine and my grandfather are in one more picture—one of the Christmas shots Elaine sent. It's the fifties—my grandparents, Elaine, her parents, my parents, and Bill, all squeezed into the living room of my grandparents' old house. I can't figure out who took the photo, who's missing. My parents are just kids—newlyweds, childless. My father and Bill are the only ones still alive from that picture.

AT MY GRANDFATHER'S FUNERAL, Bill stood outside the church smoking. He was a prison guard living in a house trailer at the time. Ex-Marine, ex-motorcycle gang member, ex-son, still unmarried. We were still *it* for him: family. I saw him brush away a tear before coming in and telling my father, "Meeting like this gets old fast."

My brother and his wife from California had made the long trek back for the funeral. He was checking in on his phone for their return flights the next day to where he now called home. It was June 6, my birthday. The next day was my nephew's high school graduation party. My brother and grandfather would both miss the parties.

Helping to clear out my grandfather's house, I grabbed one of his many toolboxes and filled it with some of his hundreds of tools. He was a mechanic for life. I loved their heft as I carried them to the car, as heavy as one of my children.

My sister stuck birthday candles in a funeral pie one of the neighbors had sent over. She lit them, and my family circled around me and sang. I blew out the candles. Kristin snapped a photo. "That's a keeper for next year's calendar," somebody said.

DELIVERING

We feel a bond with the dying flowers because
we have the sense that they are dying for us.

—Anselm Kiefer

A delivery man was frantically calling Kristin on Mother's Day, trying to find our house in rural France so he could deliver her flowers. Our children in Washington and New York had chipped in to send them through Telaflora, an international delivery service that uses local florists around the world. For us, this meant they were coming from Mimosa and Lavender, the flower shop in Saint-Paulet-De-Caisson, a small village slightly bigger than our tiny village, Laval-Saint-Roman. Laval has no commerce at all except for a winery, La Catherinette—and wineries don't really count in southern France, since they're everywhere.

I KNEW THE FLOWERS were coming, but I wasn't naïve enough to imagine the delivery would go smoothly. Satellite signals disappear in the black hole of our village surrounded by rolling hills—a dead zone for GPS, cellphones, package deliveries, repairmen, and lost Belgians who got off the autoroute prematurely in their desperation to find the south of France. Perhaps unsurprisingly, though, the water meter reader always finds us and our half-buried meter. A hand-written piece of paper with

112

our bill ends up in our mailbox, often with a little personal note like, "You might have a leak."

Few other things find their way into the mailbox, though wasps love it, constantly constructing nests inside. "*Are you going to check the mail?*" "*No, isn't it your turn to check the mail?*" After numerous angry missives from the wasps, we purchased cans of wasp killer (so large the cans themselves wouldn't fit inside the mailbox). We have the kind that freezes them to death, the kind that glues them to death, and the kind that gets them stoned.

WHAT WERE WE DOING on Mother's Day? First of all, May 8 was not Mother's Day in France—here, it typically takes place on the last Sunday in May or the first Sunday of June. But May 8 *is* V-E Day in France, commemorating the Allies victory over Germany in World War II.

On May 8, our U.S. Mother's Day, we were going to a *vide grenier* in the nearby village of Saint-Martin-d'Ardèche, on the other side of a very narrow, one-lane bridge built in 1910, across the Ardèche River from the village of Aiguèze. Each side of the bridge has a stoplight. You take turns—a distinctly French concept that we could benefit from in the U.S., the land of road rage. In France, we frequently get stuck at the red light and watch the cars drive past, waving to us as if we've done them a courtesy by obeying a traffic signal. If you are in a hurry for anything here, you're shit out of luck, or *putain de malchanceux*.

We left our car by the side of the road in Aiguèze and walked across the bridge—if you get enough of a collective mass of pedestrians, the cars will wait on both sides of the bridge as you cross. We knew the streets of St. Martin would be packed, and parking nonexistent, since the *vide grenier* was taking place in the village parking lot.

VIDE GRENIER TRANSLATES as "attic-emptier," and most villages have them in spring, in a tradition much of the world seems to relate to: Spring Cleaning! At a *vide grenier*, people are allowed to lay random junk in piles on the ground in the village for a small fee, dutifully collected by the small-fee collector, who hits up local vendors on Market Days across the globe. What he does with this money is a mystery. He wears a vest with many pockets.

For us, the *vide grenier* was an excuse to walk around and hold hands on a beautiful spring day, though, honestly, every day that spring was beautiful (too beautiful, it turns out—the beginning of a summer-long drought). Kristin, who has adapted well to all things French, walks much slower than me. I try to stay behind her so we don't get separated. The more I don't know where I'm going, the faster I walk. When our kids are with us, it works out—our daughter Rosalie walks at my pace, and our son Ramsey walks at Kristin's. They are grown, and not walking with us much anymore. They are sending flowers. It is just the two of us now, retired, trying to get back in sync. We have found holding hands an effective way to stay together these days.

THE CITY FOR OUR postal address is listed as Laval, but we live on the border with Saint-Christol-de-Rodières. Though we live in Laval, we get our water from Saint-Christol. The rusty sign on the edge of our property to announce entry into Saint-Christol has fallen and has been lying in the weeds for years next to the small bridge that crosses the *ruisseau* (small stream) that marks the border between villages. To get to our house, you turn off the main road toward Saint-Christol *before* you get to the actual village of Laval. Often, frustrated delivery drivers will call from the lonely relic of a phone booth in front of La Catherinette to shout angrily at us, "I'm *in* Laval-Saint-Roman, where are you?" Then the fun begins.

If you look up Laval-Saint-Roman on Wikipedia, you will find this, which confirms what I've just explained: "Ways of communication and transport: ⚠ *This section is empty, insufficiently detailed or incomplete*"

I LIKE THE TRAFFIC CONE—it's very French. They recognize something is amiss and indicate that knowledge with a red cone, satisfied that their work is done. My favorite French road sign is the exclamation point in a triangle, to be interpreted as you like. Just make sure it's something exciting!

A village of 213 hearty inhabitants, Laval is actually slightly larger than Saint-Christol, with 162 inhabitants (which according to Wikipedia, is because it *experienced a sharp increase in population since 1975* (itals mine)). Its inhabitants are called Saint-Christolois or Saint-Christoloises.

Inhabitants of Laval are called Lavaloise. Our villages are so small that we could easily know everyone's names, but we get these little identifiers, like team nicknames—just like Parisiens! When our friend Julien from Saint-Christol-de-Rodières—not that Julien, the other Julien—told us when we bought the house that we were now Lavaloise, pointing to the rusty sign (which was the first time I'd seen it), I thought he was joking. The only things that small that get a name in the United States are little league sports teams.

A *VIDE GRENIER* is not to be confused with a *brocante*, they say, but no one can clearly explain the difference. I'm on a mission to try and determine how a *brocante* differs from a *vide grenier*. It seems that the word *brocante* has the faint whiff of antiques, rather than junk, though they seem to have identical wares laid out by hopeful or hapless homeowners eager to get rid of stuff.

Aiguèze is one of the "Most Beautiful Villages in France"©, so they have a *brocante*. Given the official designation and signage, Aiguèze (the French love bureaucracy and creating requirements for official designations—what can be legally called champagne, for example?) is where tourists descend, zipping right past our *chemin*, not stopping in Laval or Saint-Christol, both fair-to-middling villages full of Lavaloise and Saint-Christolois. *Chemin*: typically a one-lane path on which drivers going opposite directions have to work it out—somebody pulls over where they can and lets the other car pass. Though sometimes a brawl nearly breaks out over who can be most polite.

IN ADDITION TO being a junk/garage/rummage/antiques sale, a *vide grenier* often features food and beverage vendors, and live music. Think mussels and wine, not fried Oreos and kegs of beer. This one in May was a weekend activity for locals, before tourists started arriving in June.

We had no interest in accumulating junk, given that we still are not completely sure we have actually purchased a house in France—even though the calendar suggests we did so six years ago—and thus we have not gotten out a jackhammer to drill any holes in cinderblock in order to put anything up on our bare walls. Perhaps we are waiting to find a Van Gogh at a *brocante*! We do, however, have an interest in attending any festival or fair within a short drive from our dead (not even a boulangerie!) village. The label "dead village" is problematic for me, having lived most of my adult life in Pittsburgh, where the *Living Dead* movies were filmed—I define "dead" more narrowly.

We have been to chestnut festivals, jousting festivals, olive festivals, truffle festivals, St. Valentine's festivals—St. Valentine seems to have had his bones strewn all over the countryside: his heart in Dublin, his skull in Rome, his skeleton in Glasgow, a shoulder bone in Prague. Apparently, though, there is some uncertainty about whether he's actually a saint. He may be hanging out in Saint-Limbo with Saint Patrick.

I had to dig deep to find mention of Rauquemaure, where we attended a St. Valentine festival, a town (a grand metropolis of 5,481) nearby that also claims unspecified relics. Our kids, ages two and three, seemed to enjoy it when we first came to this area back in 1997, on sabbatical from my teaching job. There isn't a holiday out there where you can't get your face painted, but just try and get a sign with your street name on it.

LAVAL ACTUALLY HAS five innovative bumpless "speed bumps," *ralentisseurs*, or *bosses de vitesse*, which I translate as "speed boss," though *bosse* literally means bump. They're bumpless because they're not bumps, but posts in the road alternating in zig-zag fashion that reduce traffic to one lane amid a series of confusing yield signs that create hesitancy and consternation as drivers either slow down or speed up, trying to take turns yet again, despite the fact that there's nothing to slow down for except the one beautiful family-run winery that dominates the main and only drag, a zero red-light town. While I have great affection for the Jouve family that runs La Catherinette (note product placement!), we are literally surrounded by other grape fields and wineries. The smell of squished grapes infuses the air in the fall. It seems unfair to call them *raisins*. It's like calling plums *prunes*, lugging along all the constipation connotations.

The speed bump has been embraced over-enthusiastically by every French village as a sign of—of what? Of being something worth slowing down for, of course. Some of them rise up like small hills, and some are optical illusions that merely look like they'll break your axle if you zoom over them.

The French enthusiasm for speed bumps is an indication that their love of the roundabout (factoid: There are an estimated 320,000,000 roundabouts in France, about 60 times more than the country with the second most, Germany) may at last be flagging. The enthusiasm for speed bumps has indeed clearly run amok. An investigation carried out by one of the journalists of the French magazine *Auto Plus* revealed that about one third of the speed bumps they analyzed around the country were, in one way or another, illegal. It's like a speed-bump goldrush.

We are considering putting a speed bump on Chemin de la Rauquette just to get some respect. If someone sees a speed bump on our long driveway, they just might think it's an actual, viable, roadway and not blow past with our packages!

IN MAY, THE WILDFLOWERS in southern France suddenly begin emerging, day by day, in wild, spontaneous eruptions, popping poppies to brighten the landscape. If it actually deigns to rain one day, the next day is bold with new color. To be honest, the idea of having cut flowers delivered seems almost absurd—the tainted luxury of them, their suffocating smell, their almost plastic sturdiness. But what was I going to tell the kids, *don't* send your mother flowers? What else could they send that might get delivered quickly and precisely on Mother's Day in a country like France, where the clocks are woozy with nonchalance?

IF YOU DO HAPPEN to get driving instructions on your device of choice, there's the fact that we live on the Chemin de la *Rauquette*, not the Chemin de la *Rouquette*, which is a *real* chemin. Chemin de la Rouquette runs through the *hameau*, or hamlet, of Rouquette, which has enough signage to send anyone looking for us with a paper map off into *Perdu*(lost) *ville*. A *hameau* is usually a few houses in a clump in the middle of nowhere. Smaller than a village, but big enough to have a name and be allowed to put up signs.

I TOLD ROSALIE to write in French "drive through gate and leave on table on terrace" in the "special instructions" box when she ordered the flowers. We'd been held hostage enough by phantom deliveries that I didn't want to sit around on our terrace listening for car tires on the gravel driveway—er, *chemin*.

The delivery man had Kristin's phone number, not mine, since she is the better French speaker. When I try to speak with her to improve my woeful French—my lack of correct, or even remotely close-to-correct pronunciation—it drives her quickly mad and she holds her head between her hands and tells me to stop talking. To be honest, yes, it might be that bad. I had to take remedial speech class for nine years in school, so even English was a challenge for me. Her joke for our French friends is that she speaks for me in French just like she speaks for me in English. I, the introvert. She, the extrovert.

AT THE *VIDE GRENIER*, we wandered the crowded, narrow streets, looking at junk that smelled like musty attic. Maybe what's different about *brocante* is that they keep their stuff in garages, not attics. A woman tried to sell me a couple of chairs—we'd been given some old, rickety kitchen chairs by our friends the Guigues six years ago, when we had no furniture, just to tide us over. Our butts are still being tided over on those crooked chairs. The woman wanted to sell me four, but we only needed two more.

Kristin's obnoxious ringtone went off. It plays a flurry of bugled hunting notes and attracts attention everywhere, even in a *vide grenier*. They hunt wild boar here, and I swear I saw some hunter-types go on high alert when they heard that ringtone. Kristin skulked away to answer the call while I worked to extract myself from the chair deal without causing an international incident. Afterwards, I found her finishing her conversation on a cement wall overlooking the Ardèche River.

She told me the kids were sending her flowers—which I knew—but that the delivery man—"We told him to put them on the table outside," I interrupted.

"He told me that," she said, "but he can't find the mailbox, the driveway, the gate, the house, or the table. I told him…." She told him all our go-to direction tricks and hacks. He was going to try again.

I FOUND SOME OLD RECORDS leaning in the shade of the village church—always a draw for me, even without a turntable here. I flipped through the stack. The guy had some Johnny Hallyday records, his face splashed across every cover. Johnny, the French Elvis, who is said to have brought rock 'n roll to France. Johnny lived forty more years than Elvis, and thus had many more phases to his career, but throughout them all, his face had the same sad, misunderstood look of ennui. The French invented ennui, after all. I was starting to feel some myself, having finally learned how to pronounce it.

KRISTIN WAS ON the phone again. It wasn't like her to miss a chance to amuse herself by looking at junk, or by looking at people looking at junk. Her anxiety was spiking at the inability to get the flowers that were circling us somewhere nearby. The look on her face reminded me of the time she lost the kids in a supermarket when they were young. She missed the kids.

THAT CALL ENDED, then another, and still no flowers.
"Why didn't we stay home?" she asked.
"That wouldn't have helped," I tried to explain. Around us, picnic benches were filling up with happy families eating and drinking and half-listening to *P'tit Jon*—"little Jon"—play an accordion and sing. Some children were dancing. One young woman bent over and began twerking against her boyfriend who, full of ennui, ignored her. Twerk. Is that a French word? *Le twerk*. They pick up a lot of American trends in France, but I believe I may have been witnessing one of the first twerks to accordion music.

KRISTIN AND THE DELIVERY MAN were talking on the phone yet again—she had her other finger in one ear to help her hear in her French ear—while I enjoyed the mad crooning of P'tit Jon, the low-budget *vide grenier* entertainer someone had rescued from an attic—at least, he seemed as happy as someone who had escaped some dark, gloomy space. He turned death metal into folk songs. He had a stoned smile, and his awful pronunciation of the English lyrics did my heart good.

At least the entertainment wasn't Luanne, who seemed to be the entertainment at every other village fete. Accompanied by this guy who was equally untalented as a guitar player, keyboard player, or DJ. The entire Luanne show was one long endless song. The drum machine never stopped while he shouted encouragement to Luanne and/or the audience—one of those guys who failed Microphone 101. He swallowed his words like a French beatboxer (*beatboxeur*). I admit, he and Luanne could get the crowd going on one particular soccer anthem that consisted of singing *la la la la la* to the tune of Gloria Gaynor's "I Will Survive." That's how I survive in France: *la la la la la*.

WHILE THIS MOSTLY Catholic nation continues to fall by the wayside on its spiritual path to the ancient church doors—except for first communions, weddings, and burials—Sunday is still a holy day of not working. If you need gas or groceries on a Sunday, shame on you. Go sit in a musty, ill-lit church and repent.

What was our guy doing, delivering on a Sunday? It will remain a sacred mystery.

KRISTIN MOTIONED URGENTLY to me. *A bientôt, Jonny Hallyday* (see you later)! The delivery man had called again, depressed and desperate—though he lived in the area, he had never heard of this magical place, Chemin de la Rauquette. Finally, the two of them came up with a last-ditch "It's crazy, but it just might work" plan. He knew where the bridge to St. Martin was, and if we could get back across the bridge to Aiguèze, he could meet us somewhere among the mess of cars bridge-side.

"How will we find him?" I asked.

"He'll be carrying flowers," she yelled.

For once, she moved faster than me as we wove our way through the dense crowd. Our kids were 27 and 29, so we'd been coming here for 25 years. They had last been to visit in summer, 2019, the year before Covid shut the world down. Our French friends had seen our kids grow up, and we'd seen theirs. Kristin spoke fluent French, and our kids learned to see the bigger world through her eyes. Our daughter is also fluent in French, and our son studied it in school for years, so they're both way ahead of me. Seasoned travelers, they wish they could spend more time with us here since we did that crazy thing and bought a house. Crazy. Very crazy. As a wise woman, who spoke from personal experience, once said to us, "Have you considered a long *let* instead of buying a place?"

THE MOTHER'S DAY FLOWERS were more than flowers—I admit, I was slow to let that sink in, surrounded by that natural sprawl of wildflowers, fruit trees budding, and the mad greenery bursting after winter doldrums. I know they're *always* supposed to be more than flowers, whether they're bought from a guy by the side of the road, or sent electronically across the ocean, but these flowers were quickly becoming everything to Kristin.

IF I WALK AROUND OUTSIDE on clear days and wave my phone in the air while uttering nonsense French syllables—or, as I call it, "speaking French"—sometimes I'll get a shaky bar on my phone and sneak a message through cyberspace—a one-word message like *Help!*

We both have French SIM cards, and dutifully do the paper-clip sex change every time we come to France, keeping the alternate chips and a bent paperclip or two in an envelope we refer to as *l'enveloppe*. Why do the French give it two p's? Try to call me at my French number and I'll explain it to you.

BECAUSE OF THE *VIDE GRENIER* and because Aiguèze is a walking village that bans traffic, and because the French will park almost anywhere, the side of the road near the bridge was clogged with haphazardly parked cars and throngs of people—at least 209—traveling in clustered waves into and out of the village. We were panicked, worried we'd never find him, that he'd given up.

Then, the seas parted: Kristin saw the man with the flowers. The man with the flowers saw her, and her look said *Those are mine!* They ran toward each other like slow-motion movie lovers reuniting after the war, any war. Seeing them on their mission, people gave them room. I ran behind, nobody budging for the agitated American repeating *pardon, pardon*, as if asking forgiveness for a host of unspeakable mortal sins.

The florist, shy, abashed, and out of breath, handed over the huge, bright bouquet, the flowers thick and sturdy in their white wrapping paper—the kids hadn't skimped. A huge smile, equally bright, on his face. I was going to say a smile of relief, but it seemed more than that—a smile of joy. *Voilà*. A French word that's become an English word (though we often misspell it), it means "to express satisfaction or approval, or to suggest an appearance as if by magic." Mission accomplished, yes, but a magic mission of love! Was he blushing? I witnessed their odd marriage. I blessed the bride. The three of us stood on the edge of the road amid the surrounding chaos. I almost said, "I now pronounce you man and wife," but I knew I'd bungle it in French. After an awkward moment of glowing silence, it was all over.

THERE'S THE *RAUQUETTE/ROUQUETTE* confusion, along with the fact that our Laval house is actually on the main road to Saint-Christol, and there is no road sign anywhere that says *Chemin de la Rauquette*. Our "chemin" is a driveway that splits: one side goes to our neighbors, and the other goes to our house. We are not big enough to be on a *chemin* or in a *hameau*— both pretty low standards to meet. We are two houses with a long, shared driveway. Our neighbor Alain keeps jazzing up his mailbox in hopes that the delivery trucks won't blow right past. He had the house number burned onto a large round cut of a tree trunk and screwed into the post below his newly-painted bright blue mailbox: *140!*

You go, Alain! Next, he'll have flashing lights and a public address system to call out to any trucks in the vicinity.

The name of our *chemin* exists only in the mind of our local mailwoman, Genevieve, who I once danced with at the village *fête*, the Fête du Rose (sponsored by our favorite winery, La

Catherinette!) after we'd both had a few glasses. Genevieve once came to the States to see her friend Mickey Mouse and eat the Grand Slam breakfast at her friend Denny's. Like many of our neighbors, she asked us boldly, "You are Americans. Why are you here?"

This is a question we are still trying to answer. As the only Americans in the vicinity, we are officially named "The Americans" until another one gets lost and ends up finding refuge here. The trip from the U.S. can take three days, particularly—as happened to us once—if you end up spending the first night further away from France than you started (in a hotel near O'Hare airport in Chicago, after starting out on a Pittsburgh to Dallas flight (long, sad story)) involving trains, planes, and automobiles, and a shuttle bus or two, and a friend on each end dropping us off or picking us up.

"Pennsylvania, where is that?"

"Close to New York," we say.

Genevieve shrugs. She knows where 136 Chemin de la Rauquette is, and that's all that matters to us. If any of our meager mail does trickle down to her, she will gladly and promptly brave the wasps and deliver it.

TRYING TO GET a package of any kind delivered is a foolish endeavor. Yet we persist. If you are waiting for a replacement credit card, as I was a couple of years ago, forget it. You can track it via FedEx as it goes back and forth from De Gaulle airport in Paris to a package center in Montpellier, then to a delivery van that hopelessly circles your postal code before giving up and shipping it back to some dark room in the airport where it is labeled as undeliverable. It was like following Santa's sleigh on Christmas Eve—it somehow never showed up on the map anywhere near our house.

If you are waiting for the airlines to deliver your lost luggage after switching airlines after canceled flights and ending up *in Chicago* (yes, that trip), then you should make yourself comfortable in your dirty clothes, leaning against Alain's slice of tree trunk. My French neighbors still talk about my homemade cardboard sign taped to our mailbox on the road: VALISE ICI DANIELS 136 CHEMIN DE LA RAUQUETTE!

KRISTIN HAD HER FLOWERS! We sunk into an awkward embrace, the bouquet caught between us. Now, where was our car parked?

We wandered back into Aiguèze, side by side, Kristin clutching her flowers in one arm as I clutched her other hand. We walked through the village—in the direction of the cemetery, we realized—people bowing as if they knew our solemn mission: to put those flowers on the grave of a national hero on V-E Day. Here, where every village, no matter how small, has its war memorials, where blood was shed in close proximity, the world wars still cast their long shadows of loss.

When we stopped at a café for coffee, the flowers nearly covering the small table, refugees from the *vide grenier* looked at us, then at the bouquet spread between us on the table, and nodded sympathetically. Though we were not grieving in that glorious sunshine, we nodded back.

THE DELIVERY MAN waved and quickly disappeared back into the crowd as if we'd imagined him. But we hadn't—we took turns smelling the flowers to reassure ourselves. Done for the day, maybe he was headed home for a family Sunday dinner, a huge tradition here. Family, as in large, extended family, long tables outside, and endless hours of drink and talk and food, with usually a village promenade thrown in at the end.

Families—we saw them everywhere. Before we left the café and headed back to the no-signal zone, Kristin was able to text our kids—our family—a picture of her with her bouquet.

WE GOT BACK to our small house and arranged the flowers in a vase from Jeremie, the local potter. Jeremie has a tacky, innocent style, like a child with finger paints—colorful, crude, and anything but subtle, but that large dazzle of flowers still overwhelmed Jeremie's vase in the late afternoon sun angling down onto the terrace. The wild poppies had bloomed, sprinkled throughout our fallow field like red stars. It was V-E Day after all, and they were doing their symbolic work. And we too bowed our heads for another long silent moment.

You can't really pick poppies—they're too delicate to last long in a vase. It's better to admire their bright blurry spots from a distance. I don't know the names of any of the other wildflowers around here, in English or in French, but that's okay—their beauty speaks for itself, in its own language of possibility and surprise.

Life is full of extravagant gestures. "Ah, another beautiful day in France!" I am known to say as the sun sets and the moon climbs up above the horizon to take its place. I like to think both sun and moon were looking at us from their various angles that evening and admiring Kristin's flowers. The Mistral wind blew the lush smell of the thick, cut flowers toward us, as if on command. Unlike the poppies, they did not bend to it.

Here, in this remote village, the stars always seem more intimate in their clarity, but that night, they seemed to approach us with an even deeper curiosity through the dark, brilliant sky.

WE WENT INSIDE, leaving the flowers out on the terrace to witness our days until they wilted like all cut flowers do. Like we will do. Those flowers didn't know the name of our *chemin* or *rue*, our *hameau* or *ville*, or the symbolic journey they had taken from the U.S. to France. Or that Kristin is a mother, that our children have sprouted into their adult years.

Like flowers, we are surrounded by what we cannot know or name. That day, we knew where we were, and that somebody had found us. *Voilà!* How lucky is that?

HOARDERS: THE "WANT-MORE-ISHNESS" SCALE

PART I: SPECTACLE AND SHAME

Like Rose and Margaret's house itself, this is going to be a bit of a shambles. Once you've got so much random scattering—no, that house was too small—scattering suggests things landing here and there. Suggests space between objects. In that house, no *between* existed. It was all *on top of*. Archeological layers pressed down so tight you practically needed a hammer to break them apart, like rocks I cracked open in geology class at the shale quarry, looking for fossils.

AUNT MARGARET WASN'T MY AUNT. She was the daughter of Aunt Rose, who also wasn't my aunt. They were my father's cousin and aunt, but that side of the family was so thinned out by tragedy that, besides my grandparents, they were all we had. Aunt Rose outlived two husbands and a number of fat, stinky dogs named Sarge.

You had to hold your breath upon entering their house, given the tidal wave of stench and what had become a clear lack of caring. It was like plunging into a pool of sewer water. You could either try to politely breathe into your shirt or find a reason to go into the scary basement that didn't smell quite so bad. My dad was always checking the boiler down there.

When I knew her, Aunt Margaret had outgrown or outlived any chance at a social life. She had lost two fingers in a
punch press as a young woman, working to support her mother
after Rose's first husband Bert got killed in a farm accident up
near Croswell. Rose's second husband, Henry, a hard-drinking
plumber whose voice sounded like gargled glass, moved her
back down to Detroit. He had the broken-veined red nose of
other family alcoholics, though Hank was no blood relation.
He died when I was a junior in high school and had recently
figured out he was a big boozer, just as I myself was blithely
drifting down that same woozy street. All roads led to the "beer
garden" for old Henry—for years, I thought it was a place that
grew beer. After he broke his leg in a fall coming home from
the garden, Sarge licked his leg cast as he slept, passed out in
his La-Z-Boy knockoff. It was the first cast I ever signed.

Rose never sold the farm. She rented it out to a soybean
farmer who sent her a monthly check. Rose cashed the checks
and never went back. Instead, she spent the rest of her life
cooking and sewing in their tiny home on the edge of Detroit.
One of the many round rag rugs she had given us was accented
with strips of my old red bathrobe. My dog Prince died on that
rug. I kept it for a long time afterwards at the foot of my bed.
If it smelled bad, I couldn't tell.

SINCE MARGARET NEVER MARRIED, and she was Rose's only
child, they got invited to our house at the holidays. I don't
remember Henry ever coming with them. Rose lived twenty
more years with Margaret after he died, but even when he was
alive, we rarely saw him. When he died, there was no official
sigh of relief, but many unofficial ones—did Rose and Margaret ever talk about running off, leaving Henry? How much
did they depend on him for money? Given that his death sent
them into a quicksand spiral that pulled all of their belongings
down on top of them, those sighs may have been better saved
for entering their house, the house of hoarders. In the days

of rotary dial phones, Margaret's must have been on a golden list that preyed on old people who had no one to talk to. Who always answered their phones and their doors and were polite and had a credit card handy.

Hoarders. Okay, that's a pejorative label. But on the Hoarder Scale, Rose and Margaret were an eleven. As the originator of the Hoarder Scale, having cleared out the homes of four hoarder relatives, including my grandfather's, my father, entitled to his opinion, might say, "Eleven? More like 11,000." Though he did get rewarded once when he found Margaret's Quaker Oats stock certificates in the middle of a sea of random papers piled in their bathtub upstairs. My father was half-convinced that Sarge was buried somewhere in the rubble, due to the reading of 11,000 on the Death Stink Meter—maybe Sarge *and* his Sarge predecessors. Or at least their ashes. The source of that stench was inscrutable and everywhere. Animal, vegetable, and human. It got in your clothes like pot smoke: "You smell like you've been over to Margaret's," said in both a pitying and accusatory tone.

Why did Margaret refuse to make a will, despite my father pleading with her for years? Maybe he needed to go to some funerals with her as a bribe to soften her up to the idea of her own death. He knew without a will, he'd inherit everything—all two industrial-sized dumpsters full of junk—as her only living relative. My father's too close to this story to tell it. He's been through a lot, the old man, but he has a theory, and I owe it to him to try to explain it to the world at large. It came to him in a dream-hallucination while in the years-long process of clearing out that house. You might think laziness creates shambles, that an industrious person is incapable of shambles, but he thinks they had a method to their dusty, musty madness, that Rose and Margaret fed the organism that became their house, letting it sprawl upward until it covered the entire staircase to the second floor like a sand dune, so that when Rose's sister Marie came to try and relocate from her old folks' home, they could say, "Surf's up! As you can see, Marie, sadly, there's no room for you here."

HIS THEORY SEEMS a bit extreme, though he'd grown up among the squabbling sisters, not me. Here's what I know about Aunt Marie (also not my aunt), the unwanted appendage of this story, to give some sense of why she wasn't welcomed into the family compound of her brother and sister's houses side by side in Warren:

She outlived her husband George by 32 years. Uncle George (not my uncle) was a World War I vet who had been part of the Polar Bear Expedition and had survived months fighting on the frozen far reaches of Russia after the war was in fact over. We compensate however we can, all of us. By the time he returned, Marie was in the process of barricading herself into their house in Lake Orion, and he fit in as part of the camouflage of order until he died.

She lived there by herself until the house was swallowed by her own hoarding, according to my father. She went on to live out her life in an old folks' home, then a nursing home. At various points, both places had called my father as her "next of kin." The first place told him they were evicting her and he needed to come take her and all her stuff away. She'd been stealing the other residents' clothes and personal items. No one would share a room with her.

At the nursing home, the same pungent troubles arose. With dementia, and people dying, opportunities for theft abounded. My father had to drive out to smooth things over, to plead with them to give her another chance. Perhaps bribes were involved. He returned with the station wagon full of plastic garbage bags and dumped them into a Goodwill bin (or two).

Rose and Marie's hapless brother, my grandfather, lived next door to Rose and Margaret for many years, though they rarely spoke. Polite neighbors, this brother and sister in old age, having been let down by their own personal tragedies, took comfort not in each other but in their accumulated junk. Like my father, they also lost a brother early on, Frank, who died in their father's saloon, choking on a chicken bone one Sunday morning while their father cleaned up from Saturday night. Their parents promptly divorced.

My grandfather had his own particular brand of squalor consisting of random auto parts, miscellaneous tools in triplicate, and his collection of empty gallon milk jugs to fill up and lug to his ramshackle cottage near Lake Huron because its well produced unsafe drinking water. In fact, it was a cottage he'd never return to, since my father sold it on land contract to a mid-level marijuana dealer who needed a safe house. Hoarding seems to present unlimited opportunities for imagination and delusion.

MARGARET ALWAYS WORE GLOVES, never taking them off, at least in our house. Just one more thing that was never explained to us—until she died. When clearing out the hoarding factory, we found multiple pairs, each with two fingers stuffed with newspaper to replace her missing ones. My father, who spent his working life in a Ford plant, said she blamed everything in her life on those missing fingers. Margaret was eight years older than him. Neither of his two siblings made it out of high school, and their existence had been hidden from us entirely.

Though those deaths of my phantom uncle and aunt, Jack and Katherine, were never spoken of, Margaret frequently called my father to tell him some distant relative or old neighbor had died—her hobby was obituary hunting. She collected the dead like she collected junk. She could look at dead bodies and not have to engage with them, just like the accumulated stuff.

My father had never heard of many of these dead people, and he'd tell her. I could hear it in his voice—a mix of embarrassment, frustration, barely concealed annoyance, and politeness verging on sarcasm. And grief for his lost siblings. I can still picture him talking to her on the phone, barricaded in the kitchen corner, resenting her interruption and the reminder of his loss, and that she was all he had left to call family: *Margaret, I don't know who that is. I don't know who you're talking about.* It seemed, given my father's continual denials, that she kept insisting that if thought for a minute, he would remember, and they could share the grief that they each had hoarded separately throughout their distant kinship.

She knew all the funeral homes. She clipped obits out of the newspapers (she subscribed to three of them, the two Detroit dailies, and *The Macomb Daily*, a local rag, just to be thorough) and we found some of those obits in either old *National Geographics* or *Reader's Digest Condensed Books*—these formed the pillars of the ancient temple of trash—when doing the big excavation after her death.

Margaret was, I realize now, clinically depressed, with a multitude of good reasons. After Rose died, Margaret slumped further into depression's dark cave. It may have begun with losing her father Bert when she was just seventeen. So, a dead father, a drunk stepfather, and there she was, the three-fingered woman. Maybe she had too much time to stare at that hand, the mangle where the fingers had been ripped off. Those fingers taken from her may have loosened her grip on everything else. Or tightened it. She never smiled. She chewed her lip until she created permanent indentations. With her face, she could have been a funeral director. A greeter. *Sorry for your loss. Sorry for your loss.* Did she practice in the mirror?

Growing up, my brothers and I developed the same lack of fondness for her as our father, dutifully kissing her jingly pale cheek until we stopped doing even that. As we got older, we were enlisted to drive over and pick her up to bring her over for holiday dinners, offering an arm to steady her up the icy walk. No small talk on those long short drives. She always seemed to be looking out the window like it was a TV set—passive, removed from the world on the other side of the glass.

AFTER LOSING HER FINGERS, she worked in an office at Quaker Oats until she retired. If she had any friends there, we never knew. They didn't come to her small funeral—even smaller than Rose's, though I suspect Margaret had made phone calls to pad Rose's statistics. Maybe my dad wasn't the only one on her funeral list.

Margaret ended her days as a resident in an old folks' home not far from my parents' house. It was a real house, with room for maybe five residents, run by a middle-aged Christian couple who made sure they were fed and refereed disputes over what to watch on the TV. She'd worked at Quaker Oats long enough to accumulate a whole range of company tchotchkes—vintage Rolled Oats tin cans, key chains, cereal bowls, box cutters, little statues of the Quaker Oats guy, coasters, serving trays, and, yes, racist plastic salt and pepper shakers of Aunt Jemima and Uncle Mose—all of which we dutifully tossed out the window into the waiting dumpster.

MY FATHER REGRETS that he didn't have the presence of mind to take pictures of the inside of that house before he started. On visits back home, I went over to Margaret's with my Dad to help during the years of endless disposing. Once, I just picked up a stack of books then dropped it at my feet. It made as much sense as anything in the futility of our efforts. "Why'd you do that?" he asked, but didn't wait for an answer.

I once suggested trying to clear out Rose and Margaret's place would make a great reality TV show, but somebody was already making that reality a reality. Do great minds think alike, or did the *Hoarders* creator have his own family hoarder? Maybe Rose and Margaret could have done a time-share/house-swap with them. A genius idea for a TV show—Celebrity Hoarder House Swap.

I think my father enjoyed showing off the hoarding like a tourist attraction. He couldn't believe it himself, and maybe needed confirmation from the rest of his family of how astounding it was: "I've already filled one dumpster, and you can't even tell," he'd say. Like he was a ringmaster at a freak show. Like an auctioneer on a made-for-TV movie.

It's the freak show aspect of this that repels and attracts me. Maybe it was our coping mechanism once they were gone and we were finally free to let it all out. After Rose died, Margaret never invited us inside the house. When we picked her up for some family event, she met us at the door, pulling it shut behind her. So, she knew. Some level of shame was involved.

I was young then. I am no longer young. My father, at 95, has been trying to clear out his own place after my mother's death two years ago. Their condo, to my naked eye, looks already cleared out. Each time I visit, I have to rehearse excuses for why I can't take any of his stuff. His basement is nearly empty, random items leaning here and there against the walls as part of his circle tour for anyone coming to visit. The complete opposite from Rose and Margaret's—nothing to give away, yet begging us to take it, versus everything to give away and hiding it. After my nephew took the ping-pong table top, my dad unloaded his grandparents' dining room table that had been hiding beneath it to one of my brothers. So excited about getting rid of it, he helped carry it up the stairs. You can forget the man is 95, and my brother, the survivor of a horrific motorcycle accident, sometimes does.

Golf clubs. A minifridge. Window air conditioner. Tray table. He sold his hunting rifles, which I'd forgotten he'd ever had. And Uncle George's World War I steel doughboy helmet, which I had covered with aluminum foil to wear to a Skylab party when it fell to earth in 1979. Somehow, it had survived all the moves and deaths and purges and was now available. It weighed a ton. I passed on it. Finally, he found a taker and donated to the Polar Bear Museum.

My father's also trying to get rid of all my mother's leftover eldercare devices down in the basement under what seems like the naïve assumption that he himself will never need them.

Walkers, wheelchairs, shower chairs, raised toilet seats. He's pushing for me to take them for my in-laws, who are younger than he is. Dad, you might need them yourself, I say. He's trying to give away a suitcase, assuming he'll never go anywhere overnight again. Dad, you might need it yourself, I say again, though he might be right about that one.

He drives a hard bargain, that man. Last time, I took a Yahtzee! game, though I already have one. His was in better shape. Yahtzee—a small game that could fit in even a smaller box. Five dice and a pad of scoresheets. "Sure you can't use anything else?" he asks. I take a few tarnished Christmas bulbs and the Christmas Colorforms, hardly making a dent, much less a splash in his stash. I did get him to take down the chin-up bar hanging over the stairs. He liked to hang on to stretch himself out so he didn't end up all hunched over like his one remaining friend, Leo the ice cream salesman. As my father will tell you, Leo is hunched over and has lost a few inches. Yahtzee bonus, anyone?

He shouldn't even be going up and down those stairs. Maybe we should cover them up with old magazines and unread books and cassette tapes, like Margaret did. Margaret's slippers! Must've been a hell of a slipper salesman out there. Boxes and boxes of brand-new slippers, though Margaret didn't seem like a slippers kind of lady. But how would I know, having been exiled for years on her front porch, waiting to pick her up and welcome her across the border and into my car. Does that make sense? Probably not. But neither did a ten-cassette collection of George Jones.

STUFF—MISCELLANEOUS OLD THINGS you think you might need someday, or stuff that reminds you of other stuff, or relics of people who are no longer with you. I myself recently downsized from a large, old, six-bedroom house my wife and I had lived in for thirty-five years into a condominium in an old church where we only have a small storage unit in the downstairs garage for our junk—er, stuff. Our kids, in their late twenties, live in the larger world known as Elsewhere. I kept taking pictures of their childhood things to see if they wanted them before they got tossed. They rarely said yes. Smart kids. On my computer, I saved the photos of everything I tossed, so if they want to look at it, they can. They don't.

My father hasn't touched my mother's stuff in her old bedroom. He's closed the heating vent, so it's cold and musty. Like an attic. Or a basement. He ignores the closet full of clothes, her ashes in a box beneath them.

What stays, what goes? Experts write books on how to get rid of junk—to downsize, travel light. What do they have hiding in their own basements, those experts? Some new TV guru has a show about how to get rid of stuff, but I heard she's in hot water for not following her own advice. Somebody told me the test should be: Will my kids want this when we die? For example, school art they made but have no memory of (perhaps because they consist of unidentifiable globs of paint and scribbled crayons and markers). With only slight blurring, a photo of Rose and Margaret's house might resemble some of their masterpieces.

Going through a lifetime's accumulation is overwhelming. And if you don't do it while you have your wits and some strength to lift things, forget about it—you're heading down the rusty rickety claptrap Margaret and Rose track. Watch so you don't trip trying to scale the mountainous staircase. I myself got caught in an avalanche in a premature ascent at Rose and Margaret's before we'd cleared a wide enough path.

While I was getting rid of my own things—a few of them, I admit, were taken from the Rose and Margaret storehouse (one particular gem, an industrial-strength standing fan that got us through many un air-conditioned summers), I thought of them sinking into that tiny house on a slowly deflating raft, adrift in that sea closing in on them, the waterfall spilling down the stairs until they were both sleeping on stinky couches on the first floor. Yep, no room for that Klepto Marie.

THE FOUR OF US—me, my wife, and our two kids—allowed each other one "Memory Box," one of those clear plastic storage tubs you see everywhere, to fill with, yes, some school artwork, along with photos, report cards, theater programs, etc. We more or less stuck to that. My wife and I, both writers, were also teachers, and we offloaded well over a thousand books, no kidding. Between our work offices, our home offices, and the bookcases in the living room and foyer, and our random Margaret-like stacks, we just kept loading up banker's boxes in the garage until a local used bookseller took pity on us and hauled them away, leaving us with a small check and an indescribable lightness. The ones he didn't want, we gave to Goodwill, and the beat-up ones we just tossed in the recycling bin. We've been in the condo for two years, and I haven't opened my memory box once. I say that not with pride, but with an urge to go open it right now.

FOR YEARS, MY FATHER had his eye on an old chest he'd seen in the cellar that Rose said had come over with the family on the boat from Belgium. We called it the Treasure Chest, imagining something of value—family heirlooms, like the chest itself. When they died and he inherited the disaster of that house, he waded through the huge piles of junk, weaving and squeezing his way through the maze down to the basement, where he was able to jimmy the chest open only to find it filled with rags torn into strips for Rose's famous rag rugs. This was the treasure stash—others besides us had been giving her their rags. Was it her dowry for death?

The mystery of Margaret's fingers was like the mystery of the treasure chest—mystery spiked with disappointment and shame. Margaret was born a month before her parents married, according to the records we found in that bathtub. A family secret that was just one of many, like all those little torn-up rags in the treasure chest. Ghosts can live, even in clutter. Especially in clutter. Even if torn into thin strips.

PART 2: MYSTERY AND WONDER
The Farm

After they "bought the farm," my father sold the farm. The magic rent check came every month for years, and they managed to live off of it. The farm was bigger than we knew. But somewhere on that farm a man, my father's Uncle Bert, had been trying to fix a tractor when gasoline ignited and burned him to death. We drove up there once when it briefly belonged to my father, and he gathered large stones from the edges of plowed fields, threw them in his trunk and brought them home to put around his bushes in the front yard of his small condo. These rocks are still there. Nostalgia with a function. My father had gone to the farm with my grandparents when he and his brother were boys. Two happy Detroit boys smiling, disheveled in the dirt. Margaret had photos we'd never seen, and we found them.

The Year of Cap'n Crunch's Crunch Berries

Pamela Low, a flavorist, developed the original Cap'n Crunch flavor in 1963—Low created the flavor coating for Cap'n Crunch, describing it as giving the cereal a quality she called "want-more-ishness."

When we were kids, Margaret brought us Christmas presents—usually cheap Quaker Oats-themed tchotchkes. But one year, she somehow got access to multiple cases of small free-sample boxes of Cap'n Crunch's Crunch Berries. For months, they appeared in our cupboard at home. What a genius idea to create an imaginary berry so that even the fruit on your cereal was unhealthy! Our parents never bought us sweetened cereal, so binging on those sample-sized boxes was a highlight of our youth. If there's a Sugar Scale for cereal, my dad would definitely put the Cap'n at 11,000.

We were so morose when we'd finished them all that our parents agreed to buy one sweetened cereal per shopping trip for their five already-manic children. Some of us thought for a time that Crunch Berries were real. And that Cap'n Crunch was really a captain. Did Margaret know the Cap'n? Was that her job, to grow Crunch Berries, like her step-father grew beer?

After finishing a bowl of Crunch Berries, we were ready to take on whatever life threw at us on the way to school, in school, and on the way home. We were on team Crunch Berry, lifting the empty bowl to drain it of the bluish orangish leftover milk.

The Labyrinth

The Labyrinth Wooden Maze Game is a game that teaches patience, balance, and steady, precise movements. This unique game helps improve concentration and perception while offering hours of fun…. Truly classic fun for the whole family! Compact and easy to play anywhere and by anyone, making it a perfect game for the home, classroom, playroom, or even on the go in the car.

Lies, all lies.

One year, Margaret gave us one of those labyrinth mazes for Christmas. You were supposed to be able to move a silver marble through the maze by twisting directional knobs on the sides to keep the marble from going down one of the many holes. As Chaz said in his online review: "Many places you have to tilt the playing surface a lot to get the ball moving. Yes, you guessed it, then the ball flies into a hole at warp speed. Bummer! A little too challenging for the age group. They lacked patience."

The labyrinth marble dropping into one of the holes was the sound of disappointment and shame. Kids "6 and Up" were supposed to be able to do it. The hard *plunk* of its hollow landing marked the failure to complete that twisty sentence yet again.

Frustrating and indestructible, that game hung around for years. Why, why could we not twist the knobs in sync to weave the marble through the maze? We relegated it to the unreachable top shelf on our basement toy cabinet. And someone lost the silver ball-bearing to boot. Oops! Some things were unattainable. Some things disappeared suddenly. You had to plug up all those holes to stay alive, right Margaret? Just weaving through the maze without the holes was hard enough without going down where the dead bodies were.

Pop-O-Matic Trouble

Then, one year, she gave us the Pop-O-Matic, a perfectly controlled game in which you didn't lose the dice, or even touch the dice, which were sealed inside the protective pop-o-matic bubble. No dice rolling on the playing surface, off the table, into the mouth of a curious dog or child. Completely safe. No Trouble at all. You just have to read the numbers and move the round plastic pegs in the round plastic holes until they all were in Home. How long did engineers work to perfect the popper so that the dice would pop up high enough to roll, and not get stuck on an edge? A genius game, truly for all ages. Indestructible. My mother kept it in the toy basket for years, and her grandchildren played it when they came to visit.

The popper never flagged. It always bounced back up. Some days when I was bored and lonely, hiding from summer heat in the basement, I'd push the popper and pretend it was talking in code to me. No batteries required.

A couple of the plastic pegs were missing, but you could improvise, like we did when playing baseball in the field out back, planting invisible runners on base when it was our turn to go in to bat again. Like stuffing paper inside the fingers of gloves you had no fingers to fill.

Oh, Aunt Margaret, we love you! Won't you play with us?

What kind of Trouble did Margaret have? First her father, then her fingers. When Rose died, Margaret breathed on her house of cards and it folded inward. She'd never cooked. Did she even know how to make Quaker Oats? When I think of her, I can still be a petulant teenager, impatient with her trembling head of white hair that was always shaking *no*. She had problems swallowing later in life. She took very small bites and choked them down. I felt sorry for her, but by then it was too late. I've learned, finally, in my sixties, that you can't wait until it's convenient to deal with old people. It's always inconvenient.

Flashback

We are eating dinner when the phone rings. It's Margaret. Rose has fallen and needs someone to pick her up off the floor. Margaret can't do it. "Let's go," my father says to me, a young man home for a visit. He gives his half-eaten dinner a longing look, then we're off. Winter, dark at 5:30, as we make the drive over the rutted icy roads of South Warren.

The last of the Sarges is still around, obese and pitiful next to Rose, pitiful herself on the floor, though she forces a smile at her predicament. She cannot hear. She is rolled on her side and Margaret has put a pillow under her head. Rose, in the process of thickening into stone in her thin house dress. The next fall will be a broken hip, and that will be that. Margaret shouts, "Ma, are you okay?" I don't check to see if she is wearing gloves.

We step into the sour smell that knocks our heads back. I haven't been inside for years, and it seems much worse than I remember. Margaret only let us inside to pick Rose up. They have to smell it. Don't they? Those downstairs couches, covered in grimy sheets. The stairway to the second floor covered, each step a shelf of some imagined orderly system, stacked with goods Margaret had purchased from friendly phone solicitors. All in their original wrappers: cassette tapes, books, condensed and uncondensed. The slippers. An authentic Veg-O-Matic, a

Ronco Showtime Rotisserie and other Ronco specials. Two salad spinners in their boxes. Endless handy household devices, impotent in their plastic and cardboard containers. Creams and bath beads from Avon. The bathtub, upstairs, on the other side of stairway mountain. The filthy downstairs toilet and sink, their only option. Still not as bad as my grandfather's next door, due to his poor aim. Oh, Grandpa, c'mon, concentrate. His own dog, Jessie, a refugee from my brother's divorce, doesn't smell nearly as bad as Sarge. What's his secret? Grandpa lets it into his fenced-in yard to do its business. No business going back there!

"Want-more-ishness" is a double-edged sword, and the duller that sword, the more dangerous. Two poor women alone in that tiny house, walls literally closing in on them. Who can blame them for taking comfort in that. Not me. Ready? We each take one of Rose's arms and pull her back into a chair, the one Henry used to get drunk in.

Wedding Bell Blues

Margaret drove out to our wedding in Pittsburgh with Elaine, my father's one other cousin. Elaine's husband had abandoned her and her infant son fifty years earlier and never returned. Another unspoken chapter in the complicated family history.

What stories did Margaret and Elaine tell each other on the long drive across the Ohio Turnpike? Or at the wedding, too old to dance, stuck at the Leftover Table of the mismatched? I bent down between them at one point during the festivities, to check in and catch my breath from vigorous dancing.

"How was the drive?" I asked.

Margaret had been drinking. She had a tiny bit of cake frosting on her upper lip. Elaine had never learned to drive. She had never been able to afford a car, and relied on Detroit's nearly non-existent mass transit system, the city having been built on the supremacy of the automobile. So, Margaret had to drive all the way, five-and-a-half hours. I don't think she'd ever left the state of Michigan in her life. Or maybe she'd made it across the river to Canada for some funeral in Windsor.

"How was the drive, he wants to know," Margaret smirked, and Elaine laughed her famous compensatory *hardy-har-har* laugh. I looked at them both. No answer was forthcoming. Margaret looked at Elaine as if they shared a deep secret. One that I would have to learn someday. I was still catching my breath. I knew at that moment that I was just a beginner. I had a wife. I had all of my fingers.

The Miracle Of The Hats

In addition to her gloves, Margaret also wore hats. Gloves and hats. Like a society woman from an earlier century. Some of the newspapers in their house were so old, they still had the Women's Section and the Society Pages.

The gloves looked pretty standard after she stuffed the two fingers with prosthetic newspapers. The hats were where she made her mad style points. On an expedition to Hoarder House one summer day, when I was in town with my wife and two young children, my father and I uncovered a treasure trove of hats: A small red plush beret. A blue felt hat that resembled a flamboyant British bobby's custodian helmet. A crushed black one that resembled a burnt pancake. An array of veiled ones just asking for some hat pins. A swirled brown one that looked like a collection of hot dog buns. Etc., etc.! Oh, hats. Hats! Even Bartholomew Cubbins would be jealous of the hats of Margaret Conroy.

I packed a bag full of them and brought them back to my parents' place, where, seeing the sun for the first time in years, those hats seemed to throb in their vibrant colors. My sister was visiting with her daughter and dog. I passed hats all around. We quickly distributed them, laughing, trying on each other's hats, instantly silly—even the dog wore one. My father, who was not silly, took a picture of us in our hats. We were standing at the gate to our yard, laughing hysterically. My mother caught open-mouthed with glee. Oh, the joy of Margaret's hats!

Were we mocking her? Were we celebrating her? That was the thing with Margaret and Rose: it was not all of one thing, or another. We hoped not to become them. My father, at 95, continues to hope not to become them. We took down his chin-up bar. Next might be his driver's license.

But at least he's getting rid of his stuff.

DEATH AND TAXES

If you carry a secret to the grave, you are holding on to that secret throughout your entire life. You are only done keeping the secret when you are dead in your grave.

My mother died on February 29, 2020. Leap Day. While approaching the next February 29, my father was still waiting for his income tax refund from the previous year. He had written DECEASED next to my mother's name on his return. That threw the whole system off, sending his return into the void for further review. Since the entire IRS was working from home due to Covid-19, which arrived approximately two weeks after my mother's death, apparently every day was now Leap Day, and perhaps in another four years my father might get his refund.

MY MOTHER'S ASHES WERE, and still are, in a box on the floor in her bedroom closet awaiting my father's death so they can go in the mausoleum together and save money—it costs every time you open the thing up. This tells you something about my father. He'll be carrying a lot of things to the grave, but his frugality is well-known, so, despite him carrying it to his grave, it is not a secret.

He threatened to send some of her ashes to the IRS to prove she's dead. My father failed to master their automated phone system, which is designed so that you will never be able to speak to an actual human being. That system works perfectly.

He said he may as well be talking to my mother's ashes. He might already be talking to them. I don't know what he does late at night, alone in their condo, when he can't sleep. Though I can't picture him digging in to scoop some into an envelope. He always curses at tax time. He sharpens his pencils as if planning to stab someone.

IN 2022, HE GOT HIS 2021 refund check, but the 2020 one was still floating around in cyberspace, far, far from my parents' condo in Sterling Heights, eight miles down the road from the house I grew up in next to Detroit. "Maybe the check's on the floor in somebody's basement," my father said, and perhaps he was right. He's never been to cyberspace and has no intention of going, though when he was 93, he did invest in his first bicycle helmet, so maybe he'll surprise us. When my well-meaning brother gave him a GPS for Christmas back when it was something you bought separately for your car, he made my brother return it. He knows where he's going.

This is the brother I sometimes call "The New Duke." "The Old Duke" is my father, a moniker given by my grandfather, who my father treated just like my brother is treating him as he's aged—with impatience and frustration.

MY FATHER'S BEEN telling me if there's anything in the condo that I want when he dies, to let him know, though he's not putting masking-taped names on the bottom of everything like my mother did. He has always been averse to clutter. My grandfather, on the other hand, had stopped caring. It seemed like he wanted to pile more and more junk on top of his heart so that no one could find it. The first Duke used to go over to Grandpa's house and do a purge, then take the trash out to the curb. My grandfather would take everything back in after my father left.

MY FATHER FILED a paper return, so he was really in for it—his return was probably in some dinosaur cave being used to start a fire. With his sharp pencils and accountant's clear numbers, my father still pays his own bills at 95 and still does his own taxes. Despite "The New Duke" trying to step in and take over. Or, perhaps *because* he is. The dining room table's covered in piles of paper—very neat piles—for at least a month every year now. Hey, it's not like he's throwing any dinner parties.

My brothers and I picked up "The Duke" thing from Grandpa and started calling our father that behind his back. When "The New Duke" bought him a sports shirt for Christmas with "The Duke" stitched on the front like it was an alligator or some other designer brand, our father gave his famous pained, constipated expression and refused to try it on, even for a quick photo. He was not owning "The Duke," the nickname for John Wayne, the actor famous for his macho swagger in Westerns and war movies. A classic tough guy, his real name was Marion, and that just wouldn't do for a cowboy/war hero.

IN OLD AGE, my father's new nickname has become "The Microwave King." He fills the freezer with frozen meals from Kroger's (one of the three places he still drives to, the others being church on Sunday and my sister's house, all within a radius of three miles), lining the boxes up like library books, using his private Duke decimal system. He picks out his daily selection from the frosty rows and zaps it at dinnertime, quite content to eat one every night. Sometimes he's in a Hungry Man mood; sometimes, it's more of a Stouffer's day.

The microwave still has the raised buttons my father created for my blind mother in order to turn it into an ersatz braille zapper. He stuck on little round furniture protectors, and they mostly worked fine. My father misses my mother, even those crazy surprises, like finding she'd placed a carton of ice cream in the dishwasher instead of the freezer.

The stove burners still have the squiggly red lines he painted on them when she still had some vision. He doesn't use the stove at all now, not that he ever used it before, except for special occasions when he'd trot out his recipe for grilled cheese: bread, butter, cheese. He still uses the coffee maker, the toaster, and the microwave—the trinity of the rest of his life.

I CALL HIM on the phone from Pittsburgh once a week, so I'm guessing he told me at least fifty times that he was still waiting for his tax return. I'll come back to that, like he came back to it—something to lean on, a clear injustice he could point to after a lifetime of unspoken or whispered injustices.

He said he wrote DECEASED in all capital letters on the return, so there should be no doubt about the fact of her death. I'm sure he did. He's always believed in capital letters. Though, actually, he didn't believe much in writing—the longest letter I ever got for him was one short paragraph, accompanied by a check. He seemed quite content to let the money do the talking. My mother wrote me weekly letters for years, and sometimes I feel like I'm paying her back with the weekly call to my father. Those letters have survived my own family's moves in my designated Memory Tub.

The Memory Tubs remind me of the empty beer cases we used as "suitcases" for our annual camping trip around Michigan—never a problem finding empty beer cases in our house. My mother painted them all some strange shade of purple with our initial on the side in white. They lined up like the six bag lunches my mother made every morning during the school year, also initialed. My dad put a board on top of the boxes, and it became my sister's bed in the cramped crank-up camper. My father still has a couple of those in his basement, paint chipped and worn, that he uses for storage. The rest of the world has shifted to plastic tubs, but "The Duke" is just fine with the beer cases.

HE DID SOMETIMES leave me notes on the kitchen table that I'd find in the morning after he'd already left for his job at the Ford factory: CLEAN UP YARD. This meant shovel up my dog Prince's shit—I tended to let the piles accumulate, and Prince was a big dog. It was a dog's bone of contention between us that someone kept digging up. To be honest, I think I liked the special attention of those notes—none of my four siblings ever got them.

Oddly enough, I never heard my father say "shit," and certainly not "fuck." He heard it all the time at work—I know, having worked at that same factory myself, where swearing was a casual kind of punctuation. Not a pious man—that'd be like bragging, which he never did—but he goes to church every Sunday. He dutifully pushed my mother in her wheelchair into the handicapped row in the back every Sunday until one day she spat out the host—out of sorts, and out of her mind. Embarrassed, he never took her back. My mother, who prayed a rosary every night (she needed no help fingering the beads in the dark), could spit out "shit" in anger or frustration with the best of them. The rest of us—we took after her in that department. My father was working too much overtime to notice.

My mother would have called the IRS on some heavenly direct line and said, "What is this shit, holding back the check because I'm dead?" My sister said she actually got a person on the line twice in her months of calling for him, but that the two gentlemen gave her completely opposite answers. Shit!

Well, at least they can't drive Dad to an early grave, I told my sister. That ship has sailed, I told her. I like mixed metaphors. My father, on the other hand, does not believe in them at all. He seems upset that *It is what it is* has become such a cliché these days, believing perhaps that he himself had invented the phrase many years ago.

HIS TAX RETURN had been flagged—it has been tarred and feathered, it made a wrong turn in Hell Freezes Over,

Nebraska—apparently because he wrote something human on the form after losing his wife of 69 years, not sticking with numbers for a computer to scan. Maybe they thought he was being sarcastic with the caps. I really can't say. He wanted to find an office he could drive to so he can complain in person. Go over the paperwork spread out on a table. Point to things with his sharp pencil.

No direct deposit for him, so on top of everything, he was waiting for a PAPER CHECK (caps mine). He uses his credit card as often as he used to use his camera: Not Very. The credit card has always been something suspicious to him. He wants to hand over the dirty, wrinkled dollar bills of his many years of hard work, not some cheap piece of plastic.

DDRING THE HEIGHT of Covid, my father dutifully wore a mask, but pulled it down whenever he wanted to speak. Or hear someone else speak. Somehow, it made sense to him. If he was paying for something—like the weekly after-church donuts—we'd stand behind him and make apologetic eye contact with whoever was working the cash register as he bent down, leaned in, and pulled his mask down to hear how much he owed.

Though I have to give him credit (with a reduced grade for lateness), he now has hearing aids. First one, then a second one! He advises anyone to get two now, suddenly the expert after years of resistance. Of course, they're always too loud or too quiet for him—too late for the mind-ear connection to even things out. Sometimes I suspect he's secretly turned them off, or down so low that the devices are only a prop to keep us from bugging him about his hearing. We got him the fancy Bluetooth kind so he can talk on the phone through his hearing aids, though twice he has tried to hand me the phone—to speak to a relative or his one living friend who now is trapped in an Arizona nursing home—before remembering you can only hear through the hearing aids. Once, he took one out and handed it over to me like a tooth he'd just pulled and wanted a dime for. "Just talk into it," he said.

Old habits die slowly, and no slower than his. He was never a phone guy, and when my mother was alive and we'd call, he'd answer, say hello, and quickly hand the phone to her.

HE COULD MAKE a roll of film last an entire year. Always a big surprise to see what was on it once he finally took it to the drug store to get developed. Some rolls had two Christmases on them. My father's reluctance to finish a roll of film was legendary—he'd get the camera out of the closet like it was a bottle with a genie inside and he only had as many wishes as were on the roll. Often, only at the insistence of our mother, who wanted at least the obligatory holiday shots—all of us in one place, standing still, which was a rare occurrence. Maybe part of it goes back to the boogieman of our childhood: the absence of our father due to nonstop overtime at the plant back when the car companies couldn't crank them out fast enough.

To actually finish a roll, knowing the inevitable dis/appointment/may/approval, etc., of the results, created anxiety for him, and he was a man rarely anxious—in the eyes of his children, anyway. He let the film stay there, spooled, safe in the dark, even once a roll was spent. Nothing could turn that tiny wound-up cocoon into a butterfly, given the ritual mugging of five goofy kids that it contained. Metamorphosis had too many syllables anyway, and sounded a lot like what had killed my grandmother.

If he didn't develop the pictures, it'd keep us alive, safe—this, I realize now, was part of the twisted logic of a man who had lost first his sister, then his brother, before graduating from high school. I didn't find out they had even existed until I was away at college. Our childhood was full of odd silences that I only understand now. Nearly everyone else I knew, adult or child, had siblings—particularly in our Catholic neighborhood.

My sophomore year of college, I went to hear Neal Shine, an editor for *The Detroit Free Press*, give a talk. I knew he'd grown up in my father's neighborhood on Detroit's East Side, so I approached him afterwards and introduced myself. He smiled and said, "Sure, I knew your Dad, but I knew your Uncle Jack better."

Uncle Jack? That explained a lot, if not everything. Sure, stories about cold, distant fathers are not unusual—a lot of Dukes out there. But I guess I'm not going with the cold, the distant. I'm going with another word that's very familiar in these times, a word "The Duke" would never use: trauma. My father was two years older than his brother, who died of a burst appendix at age fifteen. His sister, Katherine, was a Down syndrome child, though apparently this was hidden from my grandmother—perhaps by my grandfather—much longer than it should have been, until it became painfully obvious, and she was put in an institution, where she died at age fourteen.

His parents never recovered from those losses. Maybe they withheld their love from my father as a reaction to losing their other children. I do know this information, even now, is painfully sketchy. We've tried to bring it up with "The Duke," but he pleads old age and fading memory. But withhold, they did. From him, and from each other.

Stories soaked in oil, drowned. That dark odor of family silence that we took as normal. My grandfather, a mechanic at Packard Motor Car Company, engraved his initials in every tool he owned, and on all his many toolboxes. They were his jewels, his treasure chests, our inheritance—and the silence of the accumulated unspoken, beyond the years in which he could fix anything, though all the tools in the world couldn't fix what broke him.

HERE'S A STORY about my father that doesn't make sense until you know about those losses. His grandsons Matt and Jon both played football in high school. Matt, the older one, had graduated, but he came back to see his brother play in the state playoffs. Here, I'll let my father, who was at the game, take over:

"After the game, Matt went down from the stands and onto the field to comfort his brother." Here, my father's voice suddenly chokes up, and he has to pause. Then the pause lasts, and he says no more. The man who never chokes up, chokes up. A brother-memory flash causing him to shield his eyes.

MY GRANDPARENTS came over for most holidays. As kids, we sometimes spent weekends with them in Detroit. My grandmother took us to the dime store. My grandfather let us hammer nails into wood in his basement and pretend we were making boats. This all sounds like normal grandma and grandpa stuff. But it ignores the one cold room upstairs with a bunk bed in it that we were never supposed to enter, and the strange fact that my grandparents never went to church together, despite it being right across the street from their house.

My father never hugged or kissed his father or mother. He let them in the house. He took their coats, if they were wearing coats. They never exchanged gifts. If affection existed, it was sealed tight in a box, and none of us could open that package without ruining it, leaving evidence of our attempt.

My brothers and sister and I had to learn to hug and say "I love you" on our own. I can't say when we started to express those emotions. After we all left home, I'm sure of that—we created an intimacy that could not exist in that house, with his firm handshakes and disdain for any—absolutely any—public affection. It was a learned behavior to break the handshake rule—expressions of love as a form of rebellion. I don't even remember my father ever shaking his own father's hand. Maybe it was a concession from him even to shake our hands goodnight.

NOW THAT OUR MOTHER is gone and he has no one to talk to all day, he's suddenly become quite chatty. Well, he wouldn't like the word "chatty"—the connotations wouldn't suit "The Duke." All I can say is that I've had conversations lasting at least a half hour. A HALF HOUR talking to him, even if it was spent going over the tax story one more time.

MY FATHER AND HIS BROTHER JACK went to Camp Ozanam together, a free summer camp on Lake Huron for city kids from low-income families in Detroit. My sister, scouring my father's old papers, came across a letter and a postcard that they'd sent home from camp to their mother. To see my uncle's childhood printing on the back of a postcard, even scanned by my sister and emailed, choked all five of us up. It made him real, and the loss for all of us—my grandparents, my father, and us, Jack's niece and nephews—palpable.

July, 1942:

My father: "I gave Jack a postcard to write to you." The older brother taking care of the younger.

My uncle: "I am haveing a swell time. I hope everything is the same.

Your loving son, Jack"

I can't explain how just writing "Jack" puts a buzz and tremble in my fingers.

WE DROVE THE HOUR UP from Detroit to celebrate my father's 93rd birthday at an A&W drive-in out in the sun in Lexington, under an umbrella next to the parking lot. Lake Huron nearby, but we couldn't see it from beside the main street of that small town. My father doesn't own the cottage anymore, but he likes to take a drive up to go past it. He's a happy passenger now, since the distance is beyond his driving limits.

We did not sing or eat cake—not singing, our gift to the world, and to ourselves, an entire family of self-conscious obeyers, fearful of both unwarranted attention and not being able to carry a tune. The parking lot was full, and so were the tables. He had to cup his hands to hear. Maybe it was enough for him to have two of his kids—my oldest brother and I—at that round sticky table. He wore a ball cap—did I tell you he played softball in a seniors' league until he was 85? He sat up straight while eating his burger. I got a root beer float. Everything was for old time's sake, and that was perfectly okay. Our family was never right on the water. It was enough to know the lake was out there, unchanging.

Oh, sure, water levels increased, decreased, the stretch of beach expanded and contracted from year to year. On the other side, it was still Canada. We always liked Canada, crossing the Ambassador Bridge in the station wagon on one camping trip or another. Didn't we, Dad?

WE'D DRIVEN PAST the "World's Largest Yard Sale" to get into Lexington. It stretched on and on for miles down the two-lane highway. Cars parked on the shoulders, as if stopping haphazard at the scene of an accident.

We did not stop. "The Duke" has no need for any junk, extravagant or simple. His lifetime project of clearing out his own junk was in full-swing. Or half-swing. It keeps him occupied: "See anything you want to have, you know, when I'm gone?" Everything takes a long time now. Our sister is trying to save whatever evidence she can find of Katherine and Jack.

We all miss my mother. Neither my brother's wife nor my wife made the trip to Lexington. Maybe we are secretly relieved. We don't have to make small talk or large talk. The silence that we grew up with provides a kind of comfort now, out at our table beside the A&W parking lot, a soft breeze making its way up from Lake Huron. Our father is currently a connoisseur of silence. If we listen closely enough, he will explain it to us, once he stops slurping his root beer.

THE FIRST PICTURE we ever saw of my father and Jack, they were both dressed up, hair slicked back, for some high school occasion worthy of a photograph. They stood together on the street across from St. Rose, their church that sat directly across their house on the East Side of Detroit. Despite that, my uncle was always late for school, Neal Shine told me.

For years, that one photo was the only evidence—until Rose, then my grandfather, then Margaret died, and new photos emerged. I have studied and studied that picture, scanned into the "family" folder on my laptop. A couple of cocky, good-looking boys who were in it together, whatever it was.

LAST TIME I WAS HOME to visit, I fell back on the ritual, which he's always insisted on, to shake hands with him to say good-night before heading to bed—at "bedtime," back when we were kids, on nights when he was home from work. He would insist that we squeeze harder, and insisted that my own son squeeze harder when he was visiting with me while I stood silently cringing.

Were those handshakes his idea of love? I'm moving to the present now, wanting to feel his hand in mine, gripping hard (though not as hard as back when).

I'm tired from the long drive from Pittsburgh. It's time for me to sleep. I'm 67, and he's 95. His current routine is to fall asleep in his chair with the TV on. Should I wake him to say goodnight? No, not tonight.

I head up to bed in the Penthouse, the upstairs bedroom in the condo my parents moved into fifteen years ago, leaving the three-bedroom box that we were raised in, just in the nick of time. My mother's sight was failing, but she was able to memorize the condo layout, blessed with the lack of stairs to climb. We occasionally had to redirect her when she ran into walls with her walker—"Left, Mom. Now, to the right"—but she managed for many years until she could manage no more.

My father, after having had cataract surgery, sees pretty well; he's getting a little shaky at 95, and he sees that pretty clearly. He knows there will be no more film to develop. My mother put photos into albums and wrote corny captions. He never did corny. I think we all wish he did—at least once in a while—maybe he wishes it too.

I wish I could shout directions at him, but this is an unfamiliar road he'll have to navigate on his own, with no GPS. His faith in ritual and road maps remains unshaken, even as the lines fade. "I hope everything is the same." Oh, to be that innocent child.

HE'S CLOSED THE VENTS in my mother's room, so her ashes are cold. He wants no speeches at his funeral. No jokes! No peppy music! It's a funeral. It's not supposed to be fun! He wants it: "Just plain." No change-ups or modern stuff—just old-fashioned traditional silent grieving.

Please don't be hard on the old guy now—just bow your head and pray.

EXCUSE ME FOR GETTING choppy here near the end. "The Duke" would be disappointed. "Stick to the script," he'd say. The present slips into the past as I back down his driveway…

ONE TIME, HE DIDN'T stick to the script. Or maybe he planned it, though he had nothing written down. Here's the story we tell each other, to affirm that this really happened. Some days he's still "The Duke," and, frustrated, he gets angry, and stubborn, trying to provoke a showdown on Main Street about moving his chin-up bar from the top of the basement stairs—he likes to stretch out there, he says, believing it keeps him from slouching over like the old man he is. On those days, we need this story:

At their 50th wedding anniversary party, after we had all had our say, my father took the microphone and said:

One time, my grandson Patrick came up to me and said, "I love you, Grandpa." And I said, "That's nice, Patrick."

He said, "Grandpa, you're supposed to say 'I love you' back."

Well, I should have said it then, and I'll say it now, "I love you all."

"The Duke." The one and only true Duke, now and forever.

I APOLOGIZE TO HIM for sometimes referring to him in the past tense. Every time I come home for a visit, when I'm ready to drive away, he makes the universal sign for roll down your window so he can tell me one more thing. Like, *check your tires.* That's his favorite. *They look a little low.*

AT 95, HE SITS ALONE in his open garage on the wooden tete-a-tete that he used to sit on with my mother back on the front porch of our old house. The empty seat creates an imbalance, as if it's tilted by his weight. He started to re-stain it last year, but, tired of sanding, set that project aside. It looks a little rough, and it'll stay that way. Plenty of room in the garage beside the one car, the last one he'll buy from Ford's with his employee discount.

He faces the sidewalk next to the loop road that circles his condo complex so he can catch the neighbors passing by to say hello. Mr. Microwave, happy for the human connection.

If someone wants to stop and chat, he'll be happy to tell them about the tax return.

HIS FAVORITE THING is the large-scale calendar we give him every year. We started getting it for our mother as she lost her sight, but now that she's gone, he still likes filling in the large squares with his medical appointments in capital letters. When I tell him I'm coming to town, he writes down the date I'm arriving and leaving, and when I'm coming back again.

His brother, despite "haveing a swell time," never came back.

THE CHECK FROM THE IRS, on the other hand, did, remarkably, show up, a year and a half later.

That same day he drove to the bank to deposit it. FOR DEPOSIT ONLY.

ACKNOWLEDGMENTS

Special thanks to the editors and journals who originally published these essays:

"Drought," *Barcelona Review*
"Swing Set: The Giant's Footsteps," *Belt Magazine*
"The Family Calendar," *Fourth Genre*
"The Challenge Of The Sunrise," *Maryland Literary Review*
"Windblown: Recapturing the Flag," *River Teeth*
"Hoarders: The 'Want-More-Ishness' Scale," *Sepia*
"Dog/Dog," *The Tampa Review*

Thanks, also, to Waltraud Forelli and Anna Antoine at the Eschaton-Anselm Kiefer Foundation for giving permission to use the art of Anselm Kiefer on the cover, and to everyone at Cornerstone Press: Dr. Ross Tangedal, Director and Publisher, and his wonderful team: Brett Hill, Samantha Bjork, Allison Lange, Ava Willett, Sophie McPherson, Madison Schultz, and Autumn Vine.

JIM DANIELS is the award-winning writer of over twenty books, including *Gun/Shy* (2021) and *The Luck of the Fall* (2023). He is the recipient of fellowships from the National Endowment for the Arts and the Pennsylvania Council on the Arts, and his books have won four Michigan Notable Book Awards. A native of Detroit, he lives in Pittsburgh.